D1058091

Praise for
ETCHED... UPON MY HEART

"Jill courageously allows us into the rawest moments of her personal journey, and invites us to join the process by which love is defined, fear becomes faith, and suffering becomes sovereign. Undoubtedly, if 'moments are measured by depth, not by length,' then the moments that you will spend reading ETCHED...UPON MY HEART will serve as some of your most valuable."   —Elisabeth Hasselbeck, co-host, ABC's *The View*

"Jill Kelly writes with a raw honesty that is both rare and refreshing. ETCHED...UPON MY HEART will both break your heart where it needs to be broken and heal your heart at the same time."
                    —Mark Batterson, pastor of National Community Church,
                                        author of *The Circle Maker*

"I am taken...with the words in ETCHED...UPON MY HEART and the heart of the writer who wrote them, Jill Kelly. As a mother, Jill spoke to the place in me that desires to make a lasting imprint on my children's lives. As a woman, she touched the place in me that knows well of the struggle to love, lose, forgive, live faithfully, find significance. As a believer in Jesus, she stirred my deep gratitude for redemption and the God who makes all things well. There is a richness that comes from a life that has lived this, and Jill Kelly has poured her own onto the pages of ETCHED. I just read it, and I want to read it, again."
        —Lisa Whittle, speaker, Compassion advocate, author of {w}*hole*

"As I read ETCHED...UPON MY HEART, it occurred to me that Jill Kelly is missing something. Like pretense. And guile. And posturing. She swings the door to her life wide open and gives us an all-access pass to the moments that have made her. Many of those moments are sweet, but some are blindingly painful, others unvarnished and ragged. I kept meeting myself in Jill's story. Then it settled on me what the power of this book is: Jill is not telling us her story. She is telling us Jesus' story in its Jill Kelly edition."

—Jennifer Kennedy Dean, executive director of the Praying Life Foundation and author of *Live a Praying Life* and *Altar'd*

"If I had to describe ETCHED…UPON MY HEART with one word it would be *transparency*. From cover to cover are treasured moments that lead to freedom with Christ. This sweet book of memories will touch your heart as it did mine and remind you of the beautiful tapestry the Lord is writing with our lives. You will also be challenged, as was I, to invite Jesus to do a work in your own heart as you ponder your own moments through life. This book will lead you to your own intimate time to look back and see His footprints with each of us. ETCHED…UPON MY HEART shines Jesus through the life of Jill Kelly and her family where pain has led to dance. For the Lord will waste nothing with a heart willing to share glimpses of moments such as these. Moments of true life, real struggles, and victory as our heavenly Father is revealed memory by memory. What a beautiful scene to read the story of one willing to be so transparent that others might see through to the rescuer Himself, Christ."
—Shelly Wilson, Shelly Wilson Ministries

"In ETCHED…UPON MY HEART, author Jill Kelly masterfully addresses the multiple layers we hide under that keep us safe from the hard issues of life—being unloved, feeling insignificant, harboring resentment, going through suffering, unyielding selfishness, prayerless autonomy, and the dread of death. Sometimes, Jill gently removes that blanket with her pen; sometimes her writing rips the blanket off. The end result is the same: our vulnerable soul is exposed in a refreshing yet raw way and we are forced to stare at our desperate need for God. Jill knows God and the intimacy she shares with Him she willingly shares with us. But beware: it is an intimacy that has been birthed out of extreme suffering. In fact, what she writes about suffering is so profound that you will miss it if you do not discover the joy found in Christ in and at the end of your own suffering. YOU MUST READ THIS BOOK. When you do, you will discover, as I did (and as Jill wrote): God will tenderly speak to you and usher you into a deeper grace than you knew before."
—Dr. Deone Drake

Etched . . . Upon My Heart

what we learn and why we never forget

jill kelly

FaithWords®

New York Boston Nashville

Unless otherwise indicated, Scriptures are taken from the Holy Bible, New International Version®, NIV®. Copyright © 1973, 1978, 1984 by Biblica, Inc.™ Used by permission of Zondervan. All rights reserved worldwide.

Scriptures noted KJV are taken from the King James Version of the Bible.

FaithWords
Hachette Book Group
237 Park Avenue
New York, NY 10017

www.faithwords.com.

Printed in the United States of America

RRD-C

First Edition: January 2013

10 9 8 7 6 5 4 3 2 1

FaithWords is a division of Hachette Book Group, Inc.
The FaithWords name and logo are trademarks of Hachette Book Group, Inc.

The Hachette Speakers Bureau provides a wide range of authors for speaking events. To find out more, go to www.hachettespeakersbureau.com or call (866) 376-6591.

The publisher is not responsible for websites (or their content) that are not owned by the publisher.

Library of Congress Cataloging-in-Publication Data
Kelly, Jill, 1969–
  Etched— upon my heart : what we learn and why we never forget / Jill Kelly.
     p. cm.
  ISBN 978-1-4555-1427-4 (regular edition) — ISBN 978-1-4555-2245-3 (large print edition) 1. Kelly, Jill, 1969– 2. Christian biography. 3. Christian life. I. Title.
  BR1725.K433A3 2013
  277.3'083092—dc23
  [B]   2012014073

To my daughters, Erin and Camryn. Because of you, my life has been enriched in countless ways. This book is for you—so that you'll always remember and never forget God's outrageous grace and love in the midst of your "moments."

And to my mother—your continuous encouragement, love, and dedication to prayer made this book possible. Your example continues to lead me into the heart of Christ.

I love you . . . more!

"I thank my God upon every remembrance of you."

(Philippians 1:3, KJV)

contents

Introduction ix

Chapter One................love 1

Chapter Two...............significance 24

Chapter Three..............forgiveness 42

Chapter Four...............suffering 66

Chapter Five...............giving 84

Chapter Six...............prayer 103

Chapter Seven..............faithfulness 128

Chapter Eight..............death 154

One more thing before you go 180

Afterword 189

Gratitude 193

Appendix A...Hunter's Hope Foundation 197

Appendix B...16 Things I Think Jesus Would Want You to Know on
Your 16th Birthday, Erin Marie Kelly 201

Notes 207

introduction

If something were to happen to you—if today was it—what would you want your children to remember and never forget?

Loaded question. Yes, I know.

However, I figured I should probably give you a heads-up before you read on because that very question is what this book is all about.

Let me fill in some of the background.

At the time this question brashly intruded into my life, we were less than two months away from our oldest daughter, Erin, turning sixteen years old. It was a big deal to her—and to our entire family. Not so much because of all the planning involved or the fact that she would soon be driving, along with all the other fun and scary *when-you-turn-sixteen* stuff. But more so because of the many amazing things the Lord had done in all of our lives to change our hearts and reveal Himself to us.

We've been through a lot together.

Erin walked through the deep valley of heartbreak over the loss of her terminally ill younger brother, Hunter. The pain of watching him suffer for over eight years had taken its toll on Erin's heart, and yet the joy of God's presence in her life was (and still is) evident. She radiates Jesus; but even so, Erin's life is a work in progress. As her mother, there's so much I long for Erin and her younger sister, Camryn, to know. I want them to grasp and be captivated by the deep eternal truths that will change the trajectory of their lives.

I'm mindful that most of what I desire for them to know is being caught rather than taught. In other words, my kids are watching and learning all the time. And I pray that my life thus far, whether I like it or not, has been a living example or epistle, leaving an imprint etched upon their hearts every day. It's in this hope and spirit that I have tried to chronicle the spiritual heritage and highlights that have given me the perspective, passion, and vision I long to give to my girls. This book is everything I hope my daughters eventually learn, always remember, and never forget. It's everything I would share with you, woman to woman and mother to mother.

Between two covers and etched in black ink is a treasure wrapped up in moments. Moments in time that add up to a life changed by an unchanging God. Moments lived raw and wide open. But the treasure is not necessarily found in the moments or in what we learn and never forget as a result of them. Rather, the greater gift is found in the Creator of those moments and the truths we learn about Him and His character in the midst of the moments we never forget.

Etched... Upon My Heart is an extension of my soul; the heartbeat of what I have learned thus far in my journey as a daughter, sister, wife, mother, and child of God. It's an expression through defining moments, of what God has taught me about love, suffering, forgiveness, prayer, giving, death (all the themes and titles of chapters), and so much more. Believe me, I don't have this life thing all figured out. Who does? I still have so much to learn and hopefully a lot more living to do.

However, I think you'll discover that the gems found here contain untold riches. The profound and almost ordinary moments offer a priceless, much-needed, down-to-earth perspective on heavenly principles that are life altering if trusted and lived out each day. Not by any stretch is this book meant to be a scholarly thesis or exercise in what to do and what not to do. It's intensely personal—filled with the deep desires and impassioned longings I have for the two young girls I love more than words can say. As a mom, I'm sure you'll agree I need it straightforward and to the point. So what you'll find here is simple and honest, yet deeply challenging as well. Digging down deep into the moments that have shaped who you are, who God is, and who He longs for you to be is not easy. But that's where freedom, life, and everlasting peace and joy are found.

Ultimately, I hope when this life of mine is all said and done, the treasures found in the moments shared here and the heartbeat of the One behind it all will echo and remain.

Before we move on, I'm going to ask you to do something. I would like you to come away with me and bring your memories with you. And please don't tell me you have a terrible memory. That excuse is only acceptable from former football players like my husband, who suffered more concussions than he can count—or remember!

This is not some superficial memory exercise to help you blast through your past. This is about you, the God who created you, and the moments you've held on to. It's about the precious children He has entrusted into your care for such a time as this, the everyday moments—like right now. Every day you're leaving and living a legacy as your children watch you in the midst of the moments. The moments that have already come and gone—the ones that have helped to define who you are right now are also part of what has shaped you for the many God-moments still waiting to happen.

Think of this as if you and I were sitting across from each other right now; girl talk, friend to friend, and mother to mother. I've reserved the best spot in my living room for us, the brown couch in front of the fireplace.

Are you with me?

Sometimes we need an arm around our shoulders to help us see the picture the way it is instead of the way we want it to be. Because we can't move toward the way we want it to be until we see it the way it is—*it starts with real moments, in real time, with real people*. I'm going to share some very personal moments with you, but this is not meant to be a one-sided conversation. There are precious treasures waiting to be unearthed in the moments already etched upon your life. And I hope that in sharing some of mine, you'll be willing and brave enough to open up and share yours.

Saying that, I'd like to share a moment—the one that led to this book. A treasured moment in time that left me amazed by how down to earth the King of heaven really is. I took an unexpected step closer to Him that day, and maybe that's one of the best ways to view the other moments I share here in the midst of these pages—as steps that lead closer, deeper into His heart.

~

We were scurrying around trying to get everything done. Jim and his crew of buddies were dealing with the stuff guys usually take care of, while I focused on the details and decorating. It seemed like we had been preparing for this day for weeks. Erin's Sweet Sixteenth birthday party. It was two o'clock in the afternoon, and with only four hours left, there was still so much that had to be done before her guests would arrive. Centerpiece table decorations, final testing of the twinkle lights scattered all over our backyard, backup toilet paper in bathrooms (funny but true), and the tying of fuchsia-pink sashes. That's when it happened; during the tying of beautiful satin sashes. "Enjoy this moment. Right now! As you tie bows, I'm here with you. Your daughter is sixteen."

It was as if God sat down at the table right next to me. While I was feverishly tying splashes of pink all around the tent, He was there reminding me to enjoy and appreciate the moment. So right there under the white tent filled with pink sashes and sparkle, I paused. While the hustle and bustle continued all around me, I stopped and thanked God... I thanked Him for Erin, for the gift of life and breath—her life, and the blessing of every moment that God has given to our family.

And in that moment God gently reminded me that every good and perfect gift comes from Him (see James 1:17). Including pink satin sashes, the celebration of turning sixteen, sunshine when the forecast said rain, and moments that turn into memories we never forget.

Because the gift is in the moment.

And moments aren't mathematical. They aren't measured like minutes, which stretch some sixty seconds—period. No, these gifts, these moments aren't measured by length, but rather by depth. And as my son, Hunter, taught me, how long we live is not nearly as important as how deep we live.

So I believe that in reflecting upon the moments already etched, we might become better prepared to walk into the moments yet to come. The God who loves us more than we can fathom will hopefully help us to number our days...

And our moments...

That we may gain a heart of wisdom and a longing to know and love

Him more. And maybe, just maybe, we'll find that the legacy of moments we're leaving behind for our children and the generations to come clearly reflect...

A picture of the Father's heart,

The way it is,

And the way we long for it to be...

All of the moments I share here are personal. They involve real moments with real people. Some of the names in certain moments have been changed in order to respect and honor the privacy of those who were involved. The individuals who chose to allow me to use their real names have granted me permission to do so.

etched . . . upon my heart

chapter one

love

This is love: not that we loved God, but that he loved us and sent his Son as an atoning sacrifice for our sins. Dear friends, since God so loved us, we also ought to love one another. No one has ever seen God; but if we love one another, God lives in us and his love is made complete in us.

1 John 4:10–12

Who could have known it wouldn't last? My young life made sense and my belief in love was relatively intact when Jane's voice echoed through the hall that fateful day. "Jill, do you want to walk home together?"

You bet I did!

As I scrambled to gather my books, a bundle of papers erupted like a shower of confetti from the heaping pile in my arms. Grinning, Jane rushed over to help me pick them up as hordes of students mindlessly trampled through my school work.

Once we had control of the crisis, I grabbed my coat and turned to go. "Ugh, I can't believe how much homework I have tonight." I grunted as I shut my locker and then started toward the door. Jane was a year older than I was, so she understood the workload and pressure I shouldered. Pretty and popular, I looked up to her, and with the junior high school pecking order being what it is, I felt just a little bit cool by association. We talked about teenage nonsense for the first mile or so as we meandered homeward, and then our conversation changed abruptly. Why? To this day I don't know.

"You know your mom was pregnant with you and that's why she married your dad," Jane blurted out unexpectedly.

Caught completely off guard, her words pierced my soul like a serrated dagger—and it hurt.

"What?" With a jolt I stopped and immediately let her have it, my words driven by frustration and pain. Popular or not, I wanted to punch her lights out!

Fear, doubt, and shame flooded my mind, overwhelming me . . .

What in the world is she talking about? My mom? No way!

"C'mon," she fired, eyes blazing, "as if you didn't know. Jill, please. Your parents had to get married because of you."

Blood rushed from my head to my toes—I thought I'd faint and fall down right there on the cracked sidewalk. The rest of the walk to my front door seemed like an eternity, and I sure felt a little older when I got home. I don't remember anything else Jane said that day, but I'll never forget those words.

It was a beautiful September afternoon the day I began to question love.

⌒

It's hard to say when we first understand what love is. Hopefully we experience it through our parents as children right from birth, but that's not exactly the love I mean. I'm talking about the love relationship we're hard-wired with a longing for. An ache to hear someone say "I love you" and mean it. An ache to say those words to someone who will treasure them and the risk we take when we share them. We hear the words, but do we know what they mean? What is love, really? What does it look like? Feel like? Why is it so central to the human experience that it has dominated art, music, literature, movies, and more for centuries?

As a child I was certain that my parents loved me. Not because they told me so—even though they did tell me. Not because they expressed love in a tangible manner—although they did, and I remember the hugs and tears wiped away. I suppose I knew they loved me because that's what parents do—right? They love their children.

Love at an early age manifests itself in the form of security. Security in the way our parents are physically there, how they clothe us, provide shelter, and protect us. I came home to family meals, my parents attended all my activities and sporting events, they supported my very existence. I was secure, therefore, I felt loved.

Then Jane…Her words cast a gloomy cloud of doubt upon one of the most important things—if not *the* most important thing—I had believed to be true up to that point. During our walk home from school on that beautiful September afternoon, as my feet were planted on cracked sidewalk, that defining moment driven by recklessly spoken words from a teenage friend redefined me. And I began to doubt…

…the only love I knew.

I was young, naive, and hadn't lived enough life to understand love in all its purity and authenticity. I didn't know that love can't be separated from reality—where it's needed most. The Author of all that is had yet to open my heart and mind to understand and receive the truth. I would have to wait until the fullness of time, when Love Divine would reach down and rescue me. But that day, in that moment, my mind raced, pitched, and heaved—tossed on seas of insecurity. If my mother was pregnant and *had* to get married because of me, was I a mistake? If my parents *didn't* plan for me, spend moments dreaming of what life might be like for me, if they *didn't* long for their first child to be born...then maybe they didn't really want me. Maybe they didn't love me. And if they *had* to get married, well then, maybe they didn't really love each other. With questions such as these raging like a storm through my heart, my sense of security and love was far from securely battened down.

Lies.

None of what I was thinking at that time was true. It was all lies churning around in my mind, pressing deep into my heart. From that day forward, like a splinter jammed beneath my skin, those lies infected my hope in my parents' love and love in general. It grew worse with each passing day, as I carried those venomous lies around with me while their poison spread through my soul. They weighed me down, filling every emotional step I took toward relationships with fear and doubt. I didn't talk to my mother about this. When I was a teenager, we didn't talk about or even approach taboo subjects like sex with our parents. I knew I was going to have to live with this one, so I probed, pondered, and questioned love for a long time. I wondered about my parents, doubting their love for each other and for me, though they never gave me a reason to do so. Unfortunately, Jane's words were somehow stronger than the attitudes, actions, and words of parents who really did love me. My warped understanding captivated me and sent my heart careening on a wild goose chase for love—or what my fallen heart and mind thought love was.

              ✑

"Jill, my dad's not home tonight, so we'll have the house to ourselves," he said, smiling.

"Oh good." I laughed, hopping into the front seat of his car.

Gripping the steering wheel with one hand, he reached for me with the other. "I have something special planned for us," he whispered softly. Captivated by his charm, I slid across the seat to be near him. He smelled great and he was all mine—dating him had been the highlight of my young-adult experience.

"So what's the special surprise you have planned?" I asked eagerly. "You are what's special," he said with a smile, "but you'll have to wait for the surprise..." His words trailed off and filled my heart like moonlight filled the sky, and I was swept away, imagining all that might happen.

The night unfolded somewhat romantically—we watched a movie, laughed, drank, and cuddled. I wasn't old enough to consume alcohol. That's just what we all did and how could it be wrong if everyone was doing it? The movie ended and we kissed. Something was different about his kiss, however—it was rough, and I could feel his heart pounding against my chest.

I pushed him away so I could breathe.

"I'll be right back. I have to go to the bathroom," I said, getting up from the living room couch.

My radar lit up white-hot but I didn't quite understand its warning; all I had was a vague but distinct sense of danger. "What am I doing?" I whispered to myself in the bathroom down the hall. "I don't want to go back to that kiss. What am I going to do?" The smell of his cologne was all over me, making my head throb.

Startled by a knock on the door, my safe zone crumbled. "Hey, are you okay in there?"

Because he was older it was a big deal to be with him, and the pressure was relentless. As I realized where this night was going, the questions began to corner me. I can't say no this time, can I? I mean, he loves me and I love him—right? I think he does...Besides, I don't want to lose him. All the girls envy me, they want what I have—the cute older guy. I have him . . . what would it cost to keep him? Is he worth it?

After wrestling with what might actually happen in the next few minutes, I hesitantly opened the door to his eager embrace. The fear was smothering as he pressed his now-bare chest against me. I was terrified of what I might allow myself to do. Would I say yes? How far would I let him go to show his love for me? How far would my love for him take me?

"Come here," he murmured, wrapping his arms gently around my back. He walked backward, drawing me down the hall into the bedroom, holding me as close as he could.

I laughed nervously. "What in the world are you doing?" I asked as we almost tripped and fell on the floor. A small pile of dirty clothes decorated the corner of the room, and his trophies were covered with dust. I couldn't help but wonder if I'd take my place among them and soon be covered with dust as well? The clock on the nightstand glowed with the wrong time; he must have forgotten to turn it back when Daylight Saving Time ended. The navy-blue comforter on his bed was pushed against the wall, and the checkered sheets looked like they needed to be washed. He was messy.

His scent filled the room as fear filled my heart.

I swallowed hard, feeling like jagged stones were wedged in my throat, and let this boy touch me. I let him move me. I didn't stop him. I tried to believe this was where true love would be found. He was so close to me that I struggled to breathe, instinctively pulling away and trying to resist. But words fell from his mouth like rain washing over me, and I got caught up, drenched in the moment.

"I love you, Jill. I really do."

Did he really? As he tightened the gap between us, my mind exploded with fear and doubt. Is this what it's supposed to be like? I wondered. Does he really love me? Is this love for him? Love for me?

It happened in the deep darkness of the room. The clock was still wrong. The sheets were even dirtier now. And so was I.

Dirty, that's what love felt like.

Dirty.

Wrong.

Ugly.

My tears hid in the blackness of the moment as I wandered, lost, through the valley of this shadow. I couldn't see his face but heard the breathing. I felt his heart beating. This moment and its emptiness had already begun to haunt me.

I gave my love away and it was nothing like I thought it would be. Instead of embracing what I dreamed would be among the most meaningful moments of my life, I wanted to run away from his room, from his smell, from his love.

I wanted to run away from myself and the shame that now defined me.

⌐

You never forget the moment you give love away; the moment you give of yourself physically, emotionally. It's the moment you've hoped for, the moment you expect to be life changing—the unforgettable fairy-tale dream you're misled to believe has come true. You've hoped for it, longed for it, and convinced yourself that this is what real love will look and feel like. But you never ache for love more than when you're lying in the arms of the one you've just given it to, because as high as your hopes were, that's as deep as the disillusionment pierces. It was anything but what I expected. Like a thief coming to steal and destroy, what I thought was a priceless treasure turned out to be a piece of dirt painted gold—and

I bought it all, paying full price. Something immeasurably valuable was stolen from me in a moment, something I could never replace—that's what giving love away felt like for me. I'm making no excuse whatsoever, because I knew exactly what I was doing. And although I felt like I had no way out, the truth is, there was a way out—I just didn't take it. I could've walked out of that house unscathed. Untouched. I could have . . .

But I didn't. I let him in. I let the enemy school me in love.

And I discovered that sex isn't love at all. How could it be if it made me feel so disgusting and dirty? I didn't know it in that fragile moment I lay there bleeding before my emotional wounds could even begin to scar. I didn't have the heart or mind to understand the reality of this holy celebration because I didn't know the One who is Holy. The culture around me was swallowed up in immorality and perversion; immersed in the distorted, casual attitude about love, marriage, and sex. The abyss my heart had fallen into was filled with a twisted, self-gratifying expression of what the world called love. Which was the furthest thing from reality. All I knew in the resounding emptiness of that moment was that Love in its purest form had absolutely nothing to do with sexual intercourse. I didn't get it. How could I have possibly understood the beauty, wonder, and deep waters of this God-given covenant and marital expression when I wasn't even married? So I kept searching and hoping, never knowing that all the while Love was running hard after me.

⌒

It was the end of a very long day—our wedding day. The traditional Catholic service had been flawless and beautiful and the over-the-top reception provided fun for all. But now, in the haze of the early morning hours of the day after, I found myself confused and scared. Jim was passed out on the bed already, though his friends continued to party on the first floor of our suite. I could hear them celebrating. My hair, makeup, and dress were no longer picture perfect and my picture of the perfect marriage was already eroding in my heart and mind.

My best friend and maid of honor, Karyn, interrupted my troubled contemplations with a loud whisper. "What are you doing? Are you kidding me? He's already asleep? Come downstairs and hang out with us," she urged—Karyn was always ready to party.

"No, I'm good. Besides, I'm exhausted." I hugged Karyn, telling her I'd see her in the morning. As she walked away I heard someone come into the room from the entrance around the corner. Walking over to find out who it was, my mother came into the room.

"Hi, Mom," I whispered in relief, hugging her.

"I thought you might need some help getting out of that dress. How many buttons are there?" she whispered back with a smile. "What an amazing day. I can't believe Jim isn't downstairs with everybody," she said, her voice tinged with amusement.

"Yeah, I know. Shocking. From the sound of it, they're still having a blast," I responded wearily, completely drained.

"Sit and I'll help you out of that dress. You still look beautiful, Jill," Mother said, motioning for me to sit on the bed. Jim was sleeping soundly, so we spoke about the wedding in whispers, revisiting how magical and magnificent everything was. When my mother finished helping with my dress, she kissed me good night and left, quietly shutting the door behind her.

As I lay in bed next to Jim, I pondered the excitement of our wedding day.

It was all so perfect . . . or was it?

Even on this momentous day, doubt tried to cast its ugly shadow across my heart. "What in the world am I doing here?

Who do I think I am marrying an NFL quarterback?" Tears filled my eyes and cascaded down my cheeks as I continued to wonder—is this what it's going to be like? It's our wedding night and here I am lying next to my husband but I feel a thousand miles away. I feel alone. Bombarded with questions, fear, and doubt, I turned to look at Jim as he slept. And as I lay there, I tried every way I knew how to think positively about the circumstances that were now my life. But nothing helped. And so, on my first night as Mrs. Jim Kelly, I quietly cried myself to sleep.

My doubt was well founded. You see, one of the guests at our wedding ceremony was our firstborn, Erin Marie. Like my mother, I had gotten pregnant before I was married. Initially I was terrified and dreaded telling Jim, but he was as sweet and honorable as he could be. He never veered off course and was true right to the altar where I had found myself standing earlier that day—dreams in one hand, bouquet in the other. Still, I couldn't help but wonder, Does he really love me, or does he love our daughter? What if he married me because of Erin Marie? And what about me . . . It didn't last long, but on the happiest day of my life, a ribbon of doubt coiled around my heart like a snake, gradually tightening.

Would love still be ugly?

⌒

We may have been adults, but we were absolutely clueless. As much as I hate to admit it, Jim and I had no idea what we were doing the day we got married. Yes, we understood that we were making a commitment to each other, but it was the furthest thing from the covenant of love that marriage is ordained by God to be. We didn't know that then. How could we, when the true, unadulterated, pure love of God wasn't filling our hearts? And maybe for this very reason so many marriages fail and end in divorce. People enter into a covenant they don't fully understand because they don't know its Creator. Although we were sincere in our commitment, marriage was more about *finding the right person rather than being the right person.* Our self-serving pursuits drove the relationship, which is probably why everything about our marriage became more of a drain than a wellspring of life and love.

I went into marriage full of starry-eyed, idealistic expectations, and consequently found myself disillusioned and discouraged. Sadly, the expectations I had of Jim were outrageous and unrealistic. Based not so much on what I could pour into our union but what I might take from it, I heaped the crushing burden of my deep heart longings on *his* shoulders, thinking *he* was meant to fulfill them. My empty places ached to be filled, as did Jim's, but we were never meant to carry those burdens to begin with. Disappointment and frustration, unmet expectations, and drowning desires became the norm for us, dominating our routines and pushing us further and further away from each other. Unfulfilled longings continued to slowly harden my already bitter heart, and the murky shadow shrouding our relationship darkened. We lacked everything we needed in our marriage for it to even survive, much less thrive. We didn't have it in us to make it work because the God who will "work all things together for good" wasn't in the picture yet. And so we struggled for a long time, being held together by what we would later understand to be sheer grace from His heart full of love.

And it's that very love that true marriage was designed to reflect by its Creator; the love between Christ and His Bride, the Church—those who truly believe in Him. When we enter into this marriage, a covenant treasured and beautiful, as takers, soiled with the grime of our self-centeredness, we eventually find that our love is grossly inadequate to sustain our union. I'm speaking from experience. It was only when Jim and I surrendered our marriage to its Creator, allowing His selfless love to fill us, that we stopped seeking fulfillment from each other—

something no human can give another. We'd found it in Christ and consequently had the meaning, value, calling, and love we had desperately ached for, for so long. We didn't have to suck each other's soul dry, trying to take from each other what neither of us had to give.

Maybe you've experienced what I've shared here. Maybe the expectations you had for your marriage and husband have never been met. Maybe you've given up altogether. I want you to know that although you might not see it right now, there is hope for you and your marriage. There's hope that this commitment you've made can be so much more; more than you've ever in your wildest dreams imagined. When God gets involved, nothing stays the same—including your heart. And isn't that the very thing that needs Him most?

~

"Come on, Hunter, tell Mommy," Reggie said as she held my son's right hand.

He looked like such a big boy in his stander. How could this helpless babe be so full of life and joy? Without a word he speaks amazing gifts that I unwrap daily. Unspoken treasures that enrich my life beyond measure. Love that is completely unadulterated, unconditional, and pure.

Grabbing my son's left hand, I bent down so we were eye to eye. His beautiful green eyes looked right through me. In an instant I was overcome with my frailty and his faith, my weakness and his strength. Somehow, this little boy, this only son of mine, flesh of my flesh . . . somehow he understands—this thing called life and love. He spills out joy, hope, and peace so naturally, so effortlessly.

"So what's going on here, Hunterboy? I hear you have something you want to tell me. A secret. What is it, Hunter?" I asked eagerly.

"Go ahead, Hunter, tell Mommy. Tell her what we've been talking about," Reggie encouraged.

My eyes fastened on his and in a moment it happened. Hunter blinked one, two, three times in a row. Three blinks for "I love you." Time stood still as my son wrapped his silent love around me. I exploded in celebration even as my heart crumbled.

"I love you too, Hunter. I love you too," I squealed, jumping up and down in crazy celebration.

As I continued celebrating, Reggie's soft voice spoke words so true. "See, Hunter, you know exactly what's going on. You really can talk."

But he can't—yet he can. He doesn't even have to say, "I love you," because we already know. It pours out of him in full, overflowing buckets. It's spoken without words. It's felt without a touch. It's understood without explanation.

"Hunter, you're amazing! I'm so proud of you. Thank you for trying so hard. Thank you for telling me that you love me. I love you so much."

I started to unhook the vest that held his little diseased body in the stander. Once again our eyes lock and he speaks. "Blink, blink, blink..."

⌒

I thought for sure I had experienced the pinnacle of real love after the birth of our firstborn, Erin Marie. Completely overcome, I felt so full. She captivated my life in such a profound way that I honestly thought I could never love another person as much as I loved Erin.

But then her brother, Hunter, was born. On February 14, 1997— Valentine's Day and Daddy's birthday—the pride and joy of the Kelly family joined the team. The protégé son destined for greatness. The boy who would be his father's lifelong companion. With his very first breath, Hunter captured our hearts in every way. I could barely contain the joy.

Then, in a moment, a diagnosis was given...

And everything changed.

When Hunter was diagnosed with a fatal genetic disease at four months old, everything changed. Life as we knew it fell apart. When we were told he wouldn't celebrate his second birthday—that he would probably die by the age of fourteen months—the false foundation upon which we had planted our lives crumbled. Everything we understood about life, including love, fell into question.

What does love do when hearts are breaking into a million pieces?

How does love respond to immeasurable pain and anguish of heart and soul?

Like a lioness, my love for Hunter was fierce. The threat of disease would be no match for me. In the depths of diagnosis-driven despair, the fear of death made me all the more determined to display a greater love. A sacrificial love that I had never experienced nor extended before. A love that gushed out in overflowing abundance until there was nothing left to give. It would be our love for our son that would hopefully save him. We determined to go to the ends of the earth to do whatever it took to help Hunter. Nothing would we withhold for the sake of the boy.

Even at this point in time, as much as I loved, I still didn't know what real love was because I didn't know the *who* yet. The fog of desperation and gloom due to my son's suffering became the veil that God would eventually lift to show me...to reveal to me what love is...

And what it's not.

Through Hunter's unconditional love and life of suffering, God would begin to allow me to see that love was so much more than what I had understood it to be. I began to reach for it, desire it, and yet I didn't fully comprehend what it was that I was searching for. But with every heartbeat I longed for more. And instinctively, I knew something else—

I knew that I would know when I found it. Whatever that something else was, it would quench my barren, thirsty soul...

⌒

"Jill, as much as you love your children, and I know you do, you will never know what real love is until you know the love of God through His Son, Jesus." Uncle Mark spoke with grace and piercing conviction. He had been visiting often since we found out about Hunter's disease. Joy radiated from my uncle, but in such a raw moment his words hurt. Yet, unexplainably, I longed for more.

Other than the sound of bubbling water from Hunter's oxygen tank, silence filled the room like emptiness filled our souls. My mother and I were ravenous for hope, help, and healing for Hunter. With open arms and hardened hearts we struggled to grasp these words that shattered the truth as we knew it.

"What do you mean? I know I love my kids. I would do anything for them," I abruptly responded, dripping with arrogance. Mother shot me a look. She knew I was wounded, confused, and ready to contend with what I had just heard.

We were desperate, but the pain and longing that filled our hearts was stronger than the pride that entangled us—and so we listened and learned. We talked some more and Uncle Mark explained the good news. The Gospel. God's love. Sin. Separation. Redemption.

"Jill, no one can know what real love is until they know God. God is love. I'm telling you, when His love fills your heart, you'll never be the same. His love isn't what we understand love to be. It's not what we've learned from the world. He's not like us," Uncle Mark enthusiastically explained.

The living room filled with a bit of tension, yet he continued to smile and share his heart. We listened as if our lives
depended on the love-filled truth pouring out of my uncle's
heart. And even though we didn't see clearly, our eyes were
being readied to open and our hearts to receive. What is this
passion and love he speaks of? I want to know all about it. I
want what he has. I'm not even sure what it is, but just talk
of Him makes my heart race.

My mother sat on the couch near Hunter's head and ran her
fingers through his wavy brown hair. It was time for a breathing treatment and some chest therapy for the boy, so Uncle
Mark gathered his Bible and coat. As the door shut softly behind him, I realized that he may have left but the truth of
what he shared stayed with us.

~

Not long after this visit with my uncle, I surrendered my life to the Lord.
I share this life-defining moment in a later chapter. Initially, I didn't fully
grasp the deep chasm of sin's separation that God's love had bridged for
me—and for all who place their faith in Him. It was as if I was a little child, learning everything I thought I knew all over again for the first
time. Early on in my faith journey, I began to recognize the lies I had
believed about love for so long and the inertia they had. The truth about
who God is and what love is not began to fill my heart as I read His
Word and countered the lies as it poured life and truth into my mind.
Though not completely, I began to appreciate and understand that love
isn't about me; it's about Him.

And I began to learn...

God is love (1 John 4:8)

This simple yet deeply profound three-word sentence found in Scripture encompasses the rock-solid foundation upon which everything else in life rests. Love *is* not just *what*, it's *who* God *is*. We need to *get* this foundational watershed reality as if our lives depended upon it—because they do: Jesus is love. It's all for Him, all because of Him, and all about knowing and loving Him. Love itself became a man in the flesh. All mystery and glory wrapped Himself in clay. He came here to display to the world; to show you and me what Love is. What it looks like, feels like, and how it lives and loves.

Love does not exist apart from God—it is not a created entity. Love always was, is, and will be.

He's the fulfillment of our every want, need, desire, expectation, and hope. We were created by Him and for Him—a home for His love, purpose, and plan (see Col. 1:16). All that we are—the reason we live and move and have our being this very moment is to know Love—the person (see Acts 17:28). And through the knowing comes its life and expression filling us. If we miss this, we will remain empty—vacant inside, searching for love in all the wrong places and faces. We will continue aching, seeking for a love that isn't love at all. We will believe the lies, settle for the substitute, and continue to wander aimlessly through minefields of broken hearts and dreams.

Like the moments I have shared, most of us fell deep into the cesspool of the darkness and deception of the enemy's (the devil's) lies early in life's journey. Born into this world of sin and chaos we yearned for love's filling—like a heart-cry for home as we wandered about lost in a barren wilderness of sin. Our hearts were on a scavenger hunt, turning over every rock, desperately searching for the satisfaction our souls craved. We filled the empty spaces with all the garbage the world deviously dished out. From the very beginning we're spoon-fed an understanding of love that is self-seeking rather than sacrificial. Worldly rather than godly. All about getting rather than giving. And so we grow increasingly more relentless in our search for it, looking for a love that is not love at all, because everything we find just accentuates the emptiness. But even still, God is more relentless to reveal truth. To reveal Himself, and share Love in all its fullness, beauty, and reality.

A wandering heart can only find satisfaction—find "home"—in the One who created it in the first place. God created us and knows us better than we know ourselves. In Him we find provision for all that we need. We need Him. And because of love, He lets us seek and find all that love isn't. He gives us the freedom to wander through the smoke and mirrors posing as love, to seek after all that our heart of flesh craves and all the world has to offer, so that when we get to the end of ourselves and everything we think life and love should be, we find only emptiness. We end up with nothing but the deep longing for what we desperately needed in the first place—Love Himself. Simply put, we're sinners, and until we become consciously aware of our own wretchedness and need of forgiveness, we will never know real love and its Author.

The God who is love demonstrated the fullness of who He is with convincing evidence through the cross, where humanity and divinity were crucified as one. It was there that God's One and Only Son, Jesus, was slain for us while we were still swallowed up in sin: the Righteous One for the unrighteous, the Savior for the sinner, the Strong Tower for the weak ones, the Perfect, Unblemished One for the imperfect, soiled soul.

> This is how God showed his love among us: He sent his one and only Son into the world that we might live through him. This is love: not that we loved God, but that he loved us and sent his Son as an atoning sacrifice for our sins. (1 John 4:9–10)

In one of my favorite books, *Trusting God*, Jerry Bridges describes God's love in this way: "Calvary is the one objective, absolute, irrefutable proof of God's love for us."[1] The cross is the greatest expression of God's love, His character, and His identity—who He is. The tear-stained pages of human history hold no greater example of His love. Almighty God, the architect of the universe, became completely vulnerable to His creation and allowed Himself to be crucified by them so He could fill their hearts with the love they longed for.

God is love and He showed us, demonstrated for us, put action to this love—by sending His Son, Jesus, here to live the perfect life example in the flesh and die as the perfect, innocent life—lived to save us from eternal separation from God. Through God's love we receive fulfillment for our greatest need—a relationship with Love Himself.

Yet the scandalous truth is, we doubt this Love we don't even deserve in the first place.

There is nothing in us or about us as fallen human beings, given to our self-serving agendas and darkness, that is deserving or worthy of love, at least not Love Himself. And that's the incredible beauty in all of this: we don't deserve it, yet God gives us Himself unreservedly, freely, without restraint. Why? Because God *is* Love and that's what Love does.

We can't extend true sacrificial love to others until His love dwells in and flows through us. Even though I believed and felt as though I loved and poured out my life for my children, the love of Christ wasn't in me, extending from me. Our love toward others and for God, in order for it to be the kind of love we've been talking about, must be in response to His love. God's love comes first. The more we know Him, the more we love Him and the more we grow in awareness and deep understanding of our own sinfulness and utter dependence on Christ's love and what He did so graciously to reveal it. It's Christ's love for us and in us that compels us to love Him and others, including our enemies.

One of the reasons we need to know this truth as a strong and enduring foundation is because the storms of life are a given. As circumstances press in and intensify into crushing storms, the foundation becomes all-important. It's the one thing that will sustain us when much else does not. The storms of life will recognize your shelter with its visible signs of vulnerability. The shelter we've built by our own brawn and wisdom.

Why? Because God was not called upon for the most important job, building the foundation of our lives. Security is nonexistent and the word "love" is reminiscent of the vacancy sign swinging in the dirty window of an abandoned motel. Our lives, hopes, and dreams must be built on Jesus, the person, not spiritual iconography, but who He is—love in all its fullness. Everything is secondary to this—everything! Only His perfect, infinite love endures, so He must be and remain our first and all-encompassing love.

The enemy of God and His children will entice us to doubt God's love. Most often, during times of tribulation and desperation we are tempted to believe that God doesn't love us. But the truth is, God cannot be anything other than what He is and what He has described and revealed Himself to be. He cannot be unloving, just as He can never stop being God. Certainly God has revealed through Scripture that He is more than Love but that doesn't take away at all from His identity as love. This quote from A. W. Tozer might help to explain what I'm trying to say here. "From God's other known attributes we may learn much about His love. We can know, for instance, that because God is self-existent, His love had no beginning; because He is eternal, His love can have no end; because He is infinite, it has no limit; because He is holy, it is the quintessence of all spotless purity; because He is immense, His love is an incomprehensibly vast, bottomless, shoreless sea before which we kneel in joyful silence and from which the loftiest eloquence retreats confused and abashed."[2]

God cannot love us any less or any more than He already does right this very minute—or than He did when we were lost in the shadows of sin. And the crescendo of what this love looks like in all its brilliance is the cross of Christ. When tempted to doubt Love or confuse it with something it's not, all we need to do is remember and run to the cross. Having given His only Son while we were yet sinners to extend and display the depth of His love, how can we possibly doubt that God would not also be Love and extend it to us in the midst of our greatest trials and need?

"He who did not spare his own Son, but gave him up for us all—how will he not also, along with him, graciously give us all things?" (Rom. 8:32).

Digging down deep to the core of who God is reflects who we really are, allowing us to embrace Him, living Love in our deepest recesses. This is truly the bedrock of everything else shared here on these pages.

What to Remember and Never Forget...

- God is love—you cannot know what real love is apart from knowing God.
- In order to extend love to others and to God, His love must first dwell in you.
- God is love and showed us, demonstrated for us, put action to this love by sending His Son, Jesus, here to live the perfect life example in the flesh and die as the perfect, innocent life—lived to save us from eternal separation from God.
- God cannot love us any less or more than He already does right this very minute. And the extent of what this love looks like in all its brilliance is the cross of Christ.

Prayer...

Lord, it's true, You are love. I can't possibly wrap my mind and heart around this. Please give me the wisdom and understanding to know the depth of what this means for me right now, in this moment. If I have fallen for the lie that love is something other than You and what You have revealed it to be, please forgive me and help me to know and believe the truth.

With Your life in me real love is always available for me and through me. Help me to know that I am deeply and passionately loved by You. Help me to extend Your love to everyone, including my enemy and the unlovely in my life. This seems impossible, but with You all things are possible.

Help me to know and believe Your perfect love etched upon my heart. Help me to see how You have reached into the circumstances of my life to show me what Love is and what it's not . . .

Truths about Love to Etch Upon Your Heart:

For God so loved the world that he gave his one and only Son, that whoever believes in him shall not perish but have eternal life. (John 3:16)

You see, at just the right time, when we were still powerless, Christ died for the ungodly. Very rarely will anyone die for a righteous man, though for a good man someone might possibly dare to die. But God demonstrates his own love for us in this: While we were still sinners, Christ died for us. (Romans 5:6–8)

For I am convinced that neither death nor life, neither angels nor demons, neither the present nor the future, nor any powers, neither height nor depth, nor anything else in all creation, will be able to separate us from the love of God that is in Christ Jesus our Lord. (Romans 8:38–39)

Love is patient, love is kind. It does not envy, it does not boast, it is not proud. It is not rude, it is not self-seeking, it is not easily angered, it keeps no record of wrongs. Love does not delight in evil but rejoices with the truth. It always protects, always trusts, always hopes, always perseveres. Love never fails. (1 Corinthians 13:4–8)

And I pray that you, being rooted and established in love, may have power, together with all the saints, to grasp how wide and long and high and deep is the love of Christ, and to know this love that surpasses knowledge— that you may be filled to the measure of all the fullness of God. (Ephesians 3:17b–19)

Dear friends, let us love one another, for love comes from God...Whoever does not love does not know God, because God is love. This is how God showed his love among us: He sent his one and only Son into the world that we might live through him. This is love: not that we loved God, but that he loved us and sent his Son as an atoning sacrifice for our sins. (1 John 4:7–10)

We love because he first loved us. (1 John 4:19)

chapter two

significance

For you created my inmost being; you knit me together in my mother's womb. I praise you because I am fearfully and wonderfully made; your works are wonderful, I know that full well.

Psalm 139:13–14

It's cool living next to the playground—all the area kids hang out there so there's always something to do. "We're going to play kick the can and spin the bottle today. Who's in?" Bobby announces, that legendary twinkle in his eyes betraying his gruff delivery.

He's so dreamy even with dirt caked into the creases of his neck. Bobby is the neighborhood athlete and my next-door neighbor, sort of... The elementary school and tiny Baptist church are the only buildings that separate our houses. My brother is best friends with his younger brother, so I've got a sort of covert surveillance asset in place. It's only a little

schoolgirl crush but it's big enough to captivate my immature, adolescent heart. And, adding delight to the drama, my
"sources" confirm that he likes me too.

I hope he picks me to be on his team, because where Bobby
is concerned I've honed my game until I'm good enough to
make the "All-Pro" kick-the-can squad. But that's just a means
to an end, a way to get me a step closer. I feel my heart
pounding and a smile pushing its way to my face as I cross my
fingers. The truth is, I'm hoping I'll be the one he kisses when
the bottle spins around and around. I've never kissed a boy
and I desperately want Bobby to be my first kiss.

"We're in." My friend Grace points to me as she responds.

The church bells barge into my hopefully magic moment
with a dull clang that might as well be nails across a chalk-
board. That's our cue to get home for supper, but I don't want
to leave—we're having too much fun. More important, however...

There's been no first kiss yet.

As I stooped down to grab my hoodie from the ground, reluctantly admitting that I've missed my last chance to get a
first kiss, a wad of something went whizzing past my face, almost hitting me. My head snapped up so fast I nearly gave
myself whiplash looking for the source. Then, as if in super
slow motion, a large dark ball smacked Grace in the head and
inexplicably remained stuck there.

"Ouch!" she screamed, as the echo of her pain ricocheted
off the school building. To my horror, a closer look at Grace revealed a wad of burdock as big as a softball stuck in her hair.
As I moved in to try and help her, the nauseating echo of boys
snickering behind me turned my stomach.

"Yeah, and while you're trying to get that out, why don't
you wipe that dirty crap off your face?" they sneered, leaving

no doubt about who had whipped the burdock ball at my friend.

The savagery of their words pierced my heart. Shaking with anger, I could only imagine what Grace must be feeling. Before I could speak to try and comfort her, she looked up at me and, brushing off her cheeks, naively asked, "Where's the dirt?"

But there was no dirt on her face. What they mockingly called "dirty crap" was merely a birthmark. My stomach knotted up as my eyes met hers. I didn't know what to say to my friend, how to make this terrible situation better, or how to counter their unrestrained cruelty. My love and friendship just didn't seem adequate enough to trump their uninhibited meanness.

"Jerks! They're just trying to show off. Ugh! I hate them," she proclaimed, trying to pull the burdock ball out of her hair.

As I walked Grace home, I tried to lighten the mood by making her laugh. Her mother, however, was horrified and furious with those boys. They lived just two houses down from Grace's family, and her mother was ready to tear burdock-boy's door off its hinges to have a friendly conversation with his parents. Talk about a mama bear protecting her cub—future ridicule, embarrassment, and pain would not be in Grace's future if her mom had anything to say about it! She knew why they did it—they were mocking her birthmark.

⌒

Isn't it peculiar that we don't even realize something is different or abnormal until we're told it is? Like Grace's birthmark! Yes, it was obvious. Bigger than a quarter, prominent, brown, and embedded to the side of her mouth. I saw it every time we hung out. But it never bothered me until it bothered someone else—the boy I had a crush on for most of my tender, impressionable, growing-up years. As soon as I heard him say how ugly that mole was, I immediately started to contemplate the external things that made me ugly, like the birthmark on my left arm.

After leaving Grace's house that day, I ran home as if rabid dogs were snapping at my heels. Before sitting down with my family for dinner, I barricaded myself in my bedroom and stood in front of the mirror. Yanking my shirtsleeve up, I glared at the freckled mark on my arm. Suddenly, it was relevant: it diminished my value—my standing in the eyes of someone I wanted to matter to. It shot down my very "coolness"! It meant I wasn't as desirable anymore. This mark abruptly became like a troublesome stone in my shoe; it stuck out like a billboard, a repulsive defect that screamed, "Ugly!" It had to go!

I covered it up as often as I could, keeping my ugliness out of sight at all costs. In fact, I was so desperate to conceal it that I suffered through long-sleeved shirts during the scorching summer heat. I tried every trick in the book to distract others from what lay beneath my trendy tops. And when I was forced to wear short sleeves, I used makeup and whatever else I could to hide the real me. It was like a scarlet letter—a mark of inferiority buried like a land mine beneath layers of foundation. I hoped the truth stayed camouflaged, that no one would ever discover my scandalous secret: I had a mark.

Even though I could hide my nemesis, I saw what Grace endured and I lived in constant fear of being discovered. Grace's mark was on her face, so there was no way she could cover it up. Instead, she became a target, forced to live with the reckless, mean-spirited insults that followed her mockingly through the school halls. She was tough and unafraid to fight back, but the hurt and cruelty cut deep into her soul. It was about more than the mark on her face. It was about the mark deep within— the things people didn't know and couldn't see.

Eventually long sleeves and makeup weren't enough to bring me the deep peace I craved because I wasn't just covering up a birthmark. It turned out that the issue wasn't the issue at all, and my nasty birthmark

was more of a symbol, an emblematic flag of a far deeper and more desperate mark. For just as I was able to hide the mark from others but not
myself, I was also able to hide the relentless longing that echoed through
my empty soul—from everyone but myself. I couldn't pretend I didn't
feel a gut-wrenching heart-cry for love, meaning, and acceptance, or that
my life didn't bear the painful mark left by their absence.

Driven to somehow cover the unwanted stain on my soul the same
way I turned to long-sleeved shirts and foundation to cover the mark on
my arm, the net effect was the same. Despite my best efforts, all I could
do was pretend it wasn't there—cover it up and live a lie. Just as I always
knew a birthmark was beneath my sleeve and makeup job, similarly, I
knew that just beneath a very decorative surface, a vacant heart marked
my life. And because of this, it didn't take long before my value began to
seem merely decorative as well…

But the Lord let me go. He let me seek satisfaction and significance
in all the wrong places. Because, although I didn't know it at the time,
He loves me unconditionally. He knew long before I did that my failures would eventually lead me to His faithfulness. He was right there
all along, as my empty heart and jaded thinking got me lost in a wasteland of self-absorption that eventually ruined me. I convinced others and
myself that I had this life thing all figured out. And although I never
realized it at the time, my aimless wandering was part of a remarkable
plan that stayed hidden until I was no longer blind…until I could see
through His eyes and heart.

As a teenager and young adult I compared myself to the rock stars,
celebrities, magazine covers, and television ads I saw all around me. I ran
hard after all the things that the world and my hardened heart assured
me would make for a more beautiful, more popular, and cooler person
who was revered by my peer group. Unfortunately, the higher I clawed
my way up that "social food chain," crafting the perception that I had
arrived, the more my flaws stuck out and undermined my confidence.

Eventually, I took a razor to my arm, trying to cut that ugly birthmark and what it symbolized out of my life. "Go away, just go away," I mumbled angrily as I grit my teeth and dug at my flesh. A trail of blood trickled down my arm as a trail of tears cascaded down my cheeks.

I dug deeper…

Pain.

Blood.

Tears.

Seeking but never satisfied. Filling but never filled. Ever learning but never coming to the knowledge I craved. The digging didn't satisfy the deeper mark. Can pain rooted in the heart of a disillusioned girl disappear if the scandalous birthmark is dug out by the core?

No.

And neither did the freckled circle on my arm.

Although scarred over, it didn't go away—it's still there along with the inner mark. That relentless craving for purpose and meaning and the longing for something more—something other than what I am and what I know of life in this moment.

~

The wipers slapped the windshield in a weary rhythm, prying apart the angry rain that almost hid the road. I watched nervously as he lurched up against the seat and dug into his back pocket. Steadying the car through the storm's fury with one hand on the steering wheel, I suddenly missed Jim more than ever. He was out of town, and some of his friends had invited me to go out for a drink—which turned into several.

"What is he looking for?" I murmured under my breath as he continued to search his pocket. Eventually he pulled out the prize—a small bag filled with white powder. I didn't dare ask what it was; I didn't have to. I'd never actually seen cocaine before but I'd heard the horror stories, one in particular that I'd never forget. He struggled to keep the car on the road, and I struggled to keep my wits as he lifted his pinky and snorted the coke.

I thought about college and what my roommate had told me about the drug. We were in our dorm room, all snuggled up in our bunks after a night of partying at the most popular frat house on campus.

"Hey!" She stopped laughing and looked at me dead-on. "Have you ever tried cocaine?"

"No, why?" What a buzz-kill, I thought to myself. Where is she going with this? Is she going to ask me to try cocaine? Right here? Right now?

I had never tried it. In fact, I'd never even laid eyes on it. All I knew about the deadly dream powder is what I had watched on some drug-bust action movies.

"I was rushed to the hospital and almost overdosed on cocaine in high school." As she continued to share her horrifying experience of hard drug use, my buzz disappeared and I immediately became aware of two things . . .

One, I would never try cocaine.

Two, this drug almost killed my friend.

Jolted out of my momentary distraction by the sudden thumping of the car as he swerved back into the lane, I looked over at this man all drugged up behind the wheel and thought to myself, What the he%$ am I doing in this car? What if he offers me some?

He does.

"Hey, do you want some of this?"

It should have been an easy response, a no-brainer, knowing what I had been told about this drug—about the demon powder that almost killed my college roommate. But I wasn't quick to respond. Instead, I found myself actually thinking about it. Maybe if I only try a little it won't be a big deal, I rationalized. There was an intense battle going on in my mind because this was one of Jim's friends. What if I say no and he runs back to Jim with all sorts of lies like, "She's no fun, what a bore, what are you doing with her..."? It's crazy what your mind does under pressure.

◦—

Naive, scared, and impressionable, I wrestled with the offer but managed to *just say no* to the seductive white powder that night. Still, the temptation was strong. So strong that it caused me to wonder whether or not what I had learned from my dear friend was true. Cocaine can and will destroy your life if you let it.

Confused, I was trying to be someone I thought maybe I should be but wasn't—the fun, wild party girl that fits right in with the celebrity scene. But though I was tempted to be her, even *wanted* to be her—I wasn't. In fact, I didn't even really know for sure who she actually was, but I figured she liked to have fun. And "fun" probably included more than the casual drink.

The real weakness here wasn't even the drug—it was much bigger, much deeper than that. The addictions and fantasy living are simply symptoms of a much greater and more consuming need: the longing to be accepted and the desire to be the somebody we think others would rather see instead of who we really are. I didn't get this when I was offered cocaine that night, but I get it now. It's the deeper need of a heart that longs to be something else—someone people will admire or approve of.

For as long as I can remember, from the time I tried to dig the birthmark out of my arm as a teenager to my tumultuous college years, I felt like I had to compete with the girl I was supposed to be—the one who had more of what I apparently lacked.

My self-esteem and confidence continued to take one hit after another as I became Jim Kelly's girlfriend, fiancée, and eventually his wife.
I started dating Jim when I was just twenty-one years old. Fresh out of
college—naive, narcissistic, and unprepared for life. The longing to fit
some sort of Kelly-girl mold distracted and consumed me. Everything
in life became all about him; all that his life represented. I met him at
the pinnacle of his illustrious football career—the four consecutive Super Bowl years. Everyone wanted a piece of him—especially women. Yet
Jim chose me. The superstar quarterback, the famous celebrity guy who
could have any girl he wanted, wanted me on his arm. Though I looked
in the mirror and found myself still longing and completely unsatisfied,
I was eventually able to shift confidence in myself to the hopeful rescue
of the one I was with. Yet deep down I was buying into still another lie:
believing that *all I am not* will be swept up into *all that Jim is,* and *he will
become my satisfaction—my meaning.*

And so I caved in and fell for all the fleeting pleasures, worldly temp-
tations, and trappings of success. In riding the "Mrs. Jim Kelly" wave,
I embraced the facade for a false sense of security, acceptance, identity,
and value. Although this charade felt good for a while, it eventually began to starve all that was real. The unrelenting strain of trying to be
someone you're not wears you out—weakening and breaking down all
the counterfeit fronts we struggle so hard to keep up. And that's because
it's reality that nourishes our souls, not pretense. You can't survive being
someone other than who you were created to be. And you can't know
who you were created to be until you know your Creator.

Without the appropriate understanding of the signature of significance God had etched upon my life, I continued to allow my distorted
view of myself and the world to blaze my trail through life. And my
heart continued to ache right along with it. I remained restless and easily
swayed by my longing for the acceptance and approval of people. With a
soul parched and dry, I kept thirsting after something to soothe its ache,
unable to grasp what I was aching for.

I didn't know that nothing—in and of myself or of this world—would ever be able to bring me lasting satisfaction and fulfillment. I was so deeply jaded that I never even considered the truth that my eternal soul could never be filled with material dreams come true no matter how iconic they were.

During this season of worldly wandering, I couldn't think with the mind of Christ because I didn't know Him. My heart didn't beat in sync with His yet. I had no clue that there was a better way, a renewed and transformed way of thinking, living—even breathing. But eventually I would. And I'd begin to understand that it's just Jesus and His image fashioned within my soul that can support the visible portion of my life with any lasting durability and resilience. Eventually I would know and believe that the finished work of Christ on my behalf is enough—because Jesus is all that He is, I don't have to try to be someone I'm not.

Over time, I got so caught up in trying to maintain the facade, as well as fill the vast void of meaning I was so desperate for, that I eventually lost my sense of identity. And yet the truth is, I didn't even know who I was in the first place. I had yet to discover that I was fearfully and wonderfully made, created *by* God and *for* God—on purpose with purpose. My expectations and deepest desires continued to go unfulfilled, and eventually there was no one left to wrangle into my emptiness.

No one but God.

He knew I would fall for the things of this world. He knew I would be tempted to try and live apart from Him. So, out of love, He let me go. He let me dance around in the shifting shadows of this lifeless merry-go-round world. He let me go until I eventually discovered that the person I was created to be could only be found in Him. Until then, I would travel the road more traveled, I would be a follower of all that glitters but is not gold.

Rifling through the bathroom drawer for a hair band, I spot the round mirror buried under headbands and brushes. I pull out the mirror and walk over to where my son is laying in his stroller.

"Are you ready for your bath with Mommy, Hunterboy? You look all snuggled up and warm in your towel. Mommy's almost ready for you." Reggie talked softly to my son while I changed into my bathing suit in the closet nearby.

"The water is perfect, Hunter. Let's get rollin', little buddy," I say as I reach out my arms so Reggie can lay my son in them.

After a few minutes of snuggle time, I can feel Hunter's rigid muscles relax from the warmth of the water, so I start to move his legs as if he's riding a bicycle. "Someday, you're going to ride a bike. Let's see how fast you can go." If only in our imagination, we pretend like we're riding bikes together. Hunter loves bath time.

After our mile-long bike trip, I grab the round mirror sitting on the ledge of the bath and hold it in front of Hunter's face so he can see himself. He stares at his adorable face with raw wonder as I start to point out and talk about his facial features.

"Look at those beautiful, big green eyes. Just look at them, Hunter. You know that you and Mommy are the only ones with green eyes in our family. Daddy, Camryn, and sissy Erin all have blue eyes." I continue talking about the beauty that I see.

I want this only son of mine to know how beautiful and wonderful he is, just as he is. How God knit him perfectly together in my womb. I long for him to know the truth that the God of the universe saw his unformed body. He knew that Hunter would be a radiant treasure despite the disease.

After we look into the mirror and examine all the cuteness,

Reggie comes into the bathroom and asks if we're ready to get out of the bath.

"Hunter, it's time for bed. You can't stay in the Jacuzzi all night," Reggie says with joy.

"She's right, HB, your sisters are probably waiting to pray, so we better get out."

After I lay Hunter onto the beach towel in his stroller, Reggie drapes both sides of the towel around his frail, wet body. He's relaxed and ready for chest therapy and bedtime. While I dry off and get dressed, I look down at the birthmark on my arm. I stop and stare. I see the scars and I remember my friend Grace and why I tried to dig out my mark. Tears erupt with gut-wrenching force, and the next thing I know, I fall to my knees and words spill out one after another, almost as fast as my tears.

"Oh God, I'm so sorry. I'm so sorry."

I will never forget that moment. Hunter looked into the mirror. He saw himself. It crushed me to think of the many moments that I had looked into the mirror longing for something other than what I saw, desperate to change the reflection of the person looking back at me. Here was my son, completely content and thankful just to be alive.

We don't even realize the countless hours we spend in front of the mirror. It's almost an involuntary act, like breathing. But not Hunter, he had no idea what he looked like most of the time and it didn't matter to him. He wasn't looking for the marks to scrape away; they were irrelevant to his life—to reality. Other than what we had told him about his outer appearance, he had never actually brought himself in front of a mirror in order to peer into its mysteries, to see what he looked like—to check himself out. Can you even imagine?

His frail body was riddled with flaws and yet *he* was radiant. Beautiful. God used Hunter to break my heart wide open to a greater understanding and revelation. To an authentic life based on truth, a deeper hope in things unseen, and an anchor to that which would last long after my "mark" was worn away by the sands of time. Hunter taught me to live a life that seeks after the heart and esteem of God, rather than the acceptance, approval, and accolades of people. Because man looks at the outward appearance, but the Lord looks at the heart (see 1 Sam. 16:7). It's not about a name, a claim to fame, celebrity, or power; all the temporary things that give us a *false* sense of security and satisfaction. In fact, these are often the very things that corrupt and dismantle true significance.

Hunter was never consumed with the image reflecting back at him. His outer appearance was never a stumbling block or distraction. He never had to wrestle with the lies that come with living in a narcissistic, self-consumed culture. It didn't matter that his daddy was an NFL superstar. Hunter never even considered using the power of celebrity to make a way for himself. His precious life was an example that more is actually less—that the more you fill your life with wealth, fame, pleasures, temporal things, and the passing cares of this world, the less you have to fill your heart—it only makes for an empty life. In the end, all we take with us is what our hearts can hold.

Life itself was Hunter's gift, and every breath was a priceless treasure. God had intervened and shattered the tainted mirror and the image peering out of it. He opened my eyes and heart. He graciously exposed my bondage to the temporary and meaningless, leading me into a place of repentance and true freedom. God used Hunter to help me see true, authentic beauty in the imperfect, light in the darkness of disease, strength in weakness, joy in suffering, and wisdom in foolishness.

Hunter was exactly as God intended for him to be: fearfully and wonderfully made as God knit him together in my womb. God never makes mistakes; He knew the exact gene makeup that would create my son.

God wasn't surprised when Hunter was born with a fatal genetic disease. He didn't wish things had turned out differently—everything moved forward exactly the way God intended it to. He knew. It was all part of His perfect plan. God chose to use the weakness of my son to reveal His strength—our devastation to unveil His destiny.

Our loss was our greatest gain.

In letting go of all the hopes and dreams we had for a healthy son, we were able to embrace the greater glory of the God-sized dream God had for our entire family. God has a dream and destiny for you as well. He has already orchestrated all the details—past, present, and future—for your highest good, because He sees the greater vision and glory. You just need to see Him, the real thing, not your own version of God. He's not hiding—He's chosen to reveal Himself. Our significance and satisfaction can only be found in the signature of His life in ours.

⌒

Sooo…I think it's about time to throw another log on the fire, but before I do, I'm wondering if this is ringing true in your heart the way it is in mine? So let's talk. I mean really share. It's just you and me—heart to heart.

I once read a quote, though I can't remember who said it, it went something like this: "A man with an experience is never at the mercy of a man with an argument." With that in mind I have tried to avoid opinions and arguments, and instead tried to elaborate on my experiences and what they have taught me. As they say, hindsight is 20/20, right? So as I looked back, though these many trials have been hard to endure, it grew progressively easier to understand and apply their life lessons.

Consider the way God allowed me to search for value and meaning by wandering through a moral wasteland of worldly pleasures. Sifting through their empty promises of freedom, in the end all I discovered was more bondage in their lies and a scar on my arm to remind me of this. And that was His plan all along, to allow me to heap failure upon failure, allowing my desperation to grow. And as it did, it unwittingly led me right where I was aching to go—into His waiting arms where I was loved, accepted, and treasured for who I am in Him rather than who I thought I had to be!

And isn't that the web of deceit we get caught in? Whether it's the pursuit of drugs, sex, money, status, position, power, or any one of thousands of vainglories we buy into—they all wind up sweet to the taste but bitter to the belly. At the end of the day, our wandering spirits are really on the same journey I described above. The irony is that the search takes us to this place where we live the lies we embrace, even after we know we've been taken again. How many times I pretended that life was good when deep within I was empty and aching! The world didn't deliver, but all my friends were saying it did, so who was I to swim upstream crying when I could drift downstream forcing a laugh? Fame, fortune—they were all heartless lovers, so to speak. I'd fall into their embrace at night but wake up alone, snuggling with my apathy as a poor substitute.

Even in my marriage, when I placed that very burden on Jim, he couldn't set me free because he shared my bondage. And then came Hunter. In a way his body was a prison, yet he was freer trapped in his immobile frame than I was dancing with all my might. To him, the gift was in the giving, and though there wasn't a lot he was physically able to give, he gave all he had of himself—unlike me.

Still, God opened my eyes through Hunter, helping me see how enamored I had become with futility, the insignificant things in this life that really don't matter. As I said before, He used Hunter to help me see true, authentic beauty in the imperfect, light in the darkness of disease, strength in weakness, joy in suffering, and wisdom in foolishness.

And as I did, that mark on my soul—the ugly smear that stained my heart and defined me as someone who didn't fit, didn't measure up, and had to pretend—began to lose its power. I no longer had to compete with the girl I thought I was supposed to be—the one who had more of what I apparently lacked. I didn't have to pretend that the vacant heart that marked my life wasn't there beneath a very decorative surface. Quenched by truth, quenched by love, the desperate thirst that marked my life soon overflowed with a love, acceptance, and meaning that I have since been able to offer to other thirsty souls...

I think the fire is almost out; I'd better put another log on. Wow, look at the embers. All you have to do is fan them and the fire leaps to life...can you feel it?

What to Remember and Never Forget...

- Nothing in this world will ever be able to bring us lasting satisfaction and fulfillment because our eternal souls cannot be filled with material dreams come true no matter how iconic they may be.
- It is the very things that leave us empty and aching that keep us desperate, searching for something to fill us, that ultimately bring us to Christ.
- We are all marked men and women, deeply flawed and incapable of fabricating lasting meaning—we all fall short.
- Our failures will eventually lead us into God's faithfulness.

Prayer...

Lord, apart from You life has no lasting meaning or significance. In You alone I find abundance and fullness for all that my heart craves. You're everything I need right now and for eternity. Please bless me with wis-

dom and give me eyes to see and a heart to receive truth when I am tempted to fall for lies. Please help me to live out the purpose for which You created me. Remind me when I forget that I am fearfully and wonderfully made—on purpose for a purpose greater than I can comprehend.

Truths about Your Significance to Etch Upon Your Heart:

"For I know the plans I have for you," declares the LORD, "plans to prosper you and not to harm you, plans to give you hope and a future. Then you will call upon me and come and pray to me, and I will listen to you. You will seek me and find me when you seek me with all your heart. I will be found by you," declares the LORD. (Jeremiah 29:11–14)

"Before I formed you in the womb I knew you, before you were born I set you apart." (Jeremiah 1:5)

Yet you brought me out of the womb; you made me trust in you, even at my mother's breast. From birth I was cast upon you; from my mother's womb you have been my God. (Psalm 22:9–10)

For he chose us in him before the creation of the world to be holy and blameless in his sight. In love he predestined us to be adopted as his sons through Jesus Christ, in accordance with his pleasure and will...In him we were also chosen, having been predestined according to the plan of him who works out everything in conformity with the purpose of his will. (Ephesians 1:4–5, 11)

He is the image of the invisible God, firstborn over all creation. For by him all things were created: things in heaven and on earth, visible and invisible, whether thrones or powers or rulers or authorities; all things were created by him and for him. He is before all things, and in him all things hold together. (Colossians 1:15–16)

chapter three

forgiveness

"Therefore, I tell you, her many sins have been forgiven—for she loved much. But he who has been forgiven little loves little."

Luke 7:47

$\mathcal{T}$he door slams...

Its brittle echo thunders through the hushed sanctuary as a careworn man, bowed with sin's weight, struggles to melt into an unlit corner of the church. Peering out from behind the hood of his faded brown jacket and stubbled beard, the man tries to mask the darkness on his face. But like graffiti glaring from a weathered wall, it's written all over him. He doesn't dare look in my direction or risk a glance at the others waiting to confess their sins. It's a small town—we might recognize him through the cloud of guilt he's suffocating in. Unable to bear the gathering despair any longer, he bolts out the door.

My heart races as the woman kneeling next to me makes the sign of the cross and begins to rise. With my head hung down and eyes fixed on the imprint where she knelt, still pressed into the leather kneeler, I hear the clicking of her high heels as she heads toward that place. Again, the echo of that rickety old door shutting rumbles through the room and into my heart, sending chills up and down my spine. I know what happens in there—and I'm up next.

"What am I going to say?"

"Is God mad at me again?"

"Can the priest see me through that smoky screen?"

Suddenly I feel a lot like the guy in the faded brown jacket but without the five o'clock shadow. My questions are closing in on me like moving walls, enclosing my mind. And I wish I could follow him right out the door as I wait and wonder if I'll ever be good enough for God. How will I know if I am? When will forgiveness find me?

○—

My understanding of forgiveness was deeply flawed. Like many people, from a very young age I had a performance-based understanding of God's love and forgiveness. Consequently I grew up believing that if I were good enough and did enough good, then He would love me and hopefully forgive me. But I never knew for sure, and I had no idea how much good was good enough. I didn't understand the darkness of my sin in the light of God's perfection and holiness. While grace and mercy continued to be illusive, guilt and fear became my eager handmaidens. Led by their legalistic lie that I could somehow, some way earn the love of the Father, my heart was like a broken cistern, longing to be mended and filled...

With what? I didn't even know.

⌒

Her wailing pierces the darkness and jolts me from a deep sleep. My mother is crying—no, she's bawling. I jump out of bed and, tripping over the blanket wrapped tightly around my body, fumble over to the bedroom door.

"What's wrong with my mom?" I hear myself whisper to the darkness all around me. "What happened? Why is she crying?"

I long to run to her rescue, but I don't. Instead, I listen and wonder. In a few hours she'll bend down, gently kiss my forehead, whisper "Good morning," and wake me for school. I will sleep now and ask her tomorrow, I thought. But sleep eludes me, and darkness has settled in everywhere. I long for first light to dispel the shadows of my anxious thoughts. I've never heard her cry like that before, except when Grandma Emma died. What could it be? I wonder and contemplate the possibilities.

The question bursts from my lips before hers can kiss my forehead. "Mom, why were you crying?"

Her face flushes and she turns to walk away, forgetting the kiss.

"Mom?" I call, with slight hesitation and fear in my voice.

"We'll talk about it later," she responds abruptly. "Now get ready for school."

The school day drags, and though I try to concentrate on my assignments, horrible thoughts of my mother continually barge in and distract me. "What if she's dying?" The very thought of this makes me sick to my stomach. I'm listening but hearing nothing of the middle school world all around me. I'm a million miles away.

Mom and Dad are still at work when my brother Jack and I burst through the door after school. Soon the silence of our empty home is swallowed up in raucous boy sounds coming from my younger brother's bedroom—he's a typical boy. My nervous gaze keeps returning to the wall clock, hoping to see time pass much faster than it does. And though it seems like two days, in just two more hours Mother will walk through our front door and I'll ask her then. While I wait, the soothing voice of my favorite heartthrob, Shaun Cassidy, swirls about my bedroom, drowning out the questions that tug so relentlessly at my heart.

Finally she is home. I scramble to meet her at the door and gush with joy as relief rushes through me. Melting into one of her legendary hugs, I look up at her as she asks, "Where's your brother?"

I was so caught up in the dreamy world of teen music I didn't even realize that Jack had gone to play with friends until my mother and I read his scribbled letter on the kitchen table.

It's just the two of us. This is good, I thought. Now I'm sure she will tell me why she was crying.

I wait for her to change into more comfortable clothes and then squeeze both of her strong yet soft hands.

Strong yet soft, just like her heart...

Just like her!

I hold her tightly, take a deep breath, and finally ask the question that has virtually reframed my very identity over the past twenty-four hours. I'm holding on to her softness and hoping in her strength, as if to tell her that everything will be okay.

"Mom, I was wondering...um, well, I mean...Mom, why were you crying last night?"

She knows that answering this dreaded question will drain the life right out of her, so she hesitates. Her eyes fill with tears as a horrible hush seeps into the room and settles over us. Her worn expression, along with the tears streaming from her eyes, tells me this will not be good news.

And it's not.

"Your father made a terrible decision, and he . . . he . . ." She tries to explain but cannot. I wrap my arms around her and gather her as tightly as I can as she begins to weep in my arms. She's my mother. What decision could have possibly caused her this deep pain?

Slowly she explains what happened. Anger, sorrow, and confusion become my new best friends. I barely have time to compose myself when I hear my father come through the front door.

"Hello," he says.

"Who cares?" I mumble.

Angry thoughts and even swear words ricochet through my mind, but—thankfully—they don't find their way to my lips.

She goes to my father. Why? I wonder. How can she even talk to him or look at him?

My bedroom becomes a sanctuary I have no intention of leaving. Safely sprawled across my canopy bed, I dwell on the news that threatens to shatter my fragile world.

Fear . . .

Anger . . .

Loss . . .

Tears stain my pillow as the picture of the perfect family on my dresser shatters in my heart. No, we don't have a lot. But we love deeply in spite of our imperfections. The couch in the living room is covered by a blanket that hides the torn cushions underneath. And now I will hide my torn heart. How will I do this? Where will I find a blanket that can cover a nasty rip—no, a wound, like this? Forgiving him isn't even a thought right now.

It's dark out and quiet.

Alone but for the tears that softly seep into my pillow. Until...

...he comes in.

I don't look at him as he walks over to where I'm lying.

"Your mother told me that she told you."

As he sits on the end of my bed, I immediately move away and look out the window.

I don't know what to do or say.

"I didn't mean to hurt your mother." He starts to cry.

I have never, ever seen my father cry. What should I do? Should I turn to him? Anger keeps me from acknowledging anything—his presence, his tears.

"I'm sorry, Jill," he says as he moves in close to hug me.

Pain hammers away at my heart and with harsh words I lash out at my dad. "I don't want to even look at you. I hate you."

I run out of the room and then out of the house without even looking at him.

I run away into the darkness, where it wraps itself around me like a blanket.

And I hide...

From the pain and my dad.

⌒

For years, even decades, my heart does not forgive my father. I don't even know what forgiveness is. I don't know how to forgive, and so I run and hide from what I don't understand. My heart is like papier-mâché, hard on the outside but fragile and hollow on the inside. Life goes on, but I don't look at my dad the way I used to. In fact, I don't look at life or love the same way anymore either—that is, until my heart is opened wide and I begin to see through God's eyes. But right now, in this moment etched upon my destiny, I'm blinded by unforgiveness. I can't see right now. But I will. Unforgiveness has wrapped itself around my heart like a blind-fold, and every day I'm dying a little more in the dark. It seems I have much to learn about love and forgiveness. Eventually I will learn, understand, and live. As we all do, I will begin to grasp a firsthand knowledge of authentic forgiveness, its Author, what it really is, how it feels, and how to extend it.

And I will heal.

And forgive . . . and receive forgiveness.

Eventually.

⌒

A soft summer breeze nudges the canary-yellow curtain up against my leg. The yummy aroma of freshly baked raspberry pie comforts my soul and takes me away to easier days as I stare out the kitchen window.

I wonder how he'll tell them, I think to myself as I watch my husband talking to my parents out by the swimming pool. It's an absolutely gorgeous day—almost perfect, if there is such a thing. His hands are active with expression as he tries to explain.

He's asking for forgiveness.

He's been unfaithful.

He chose to do what he knew was wrong—what he knew would crush me.

And it did.

Why should I forgive him? I think to myself. He doesn't even act like he's truly sorry.

But the truth is, I don't even know what "truly sorry" is or what it should look like. In my mind's eye I see it, but it is distant and vague, and I can't make out its defining characteristics. Like an oasis glimpsed through the haze of a sweltering desert, it could be a mirage or it could be the real thing...how can I know?

Maybe when he's sorry enough, I'll forgive, but...

I'm going to wait.

Wait to see "sorry."

Wait until I can recognize it as the real thing.

Wait until then to forgive.

Suddenly that familiar feeling deep inside my chest interrupts me. Like a vise gripping my heart, I can feel it tightening, squeezing the life from me. Breathing is hard. I think some more. And I remember that day—that day when I said the h-word to my father and ran recklessly away from the pain. I ran from my father and my Heavenly Father's love into the bitter embrace of unforgiveness. I can't believe I'm in its arms again, in the grip of this moment. I should've known better. My heart stiffens.

I examine my father's facial expressions—probing, exploring, wondering what he's thinking; what he's going to say. Will he forgive? Certainly he should know how Jim must feel. Mother's back is facing me so I cannot see her responses or read her expressions. She knows how I feel; she's been where I am right now. I bet she's crying. Crying for me and with me as she remembers how it felt when hurt like this cut deep into her heart. Finally the conversation ends, and we eat lunch together in awkward silence.

Blank.

Empty.

Confused.

How do we act like nothing happened when our hearts are bleeding all over the place? We're falling to pieces with only the silence to help keep us together.

Because I still didn't fully understand forgiveness yet, I began to measure and evaluate it with action. Based upon my deeply flawed, performance-based measuring stick, I determined to wait for what I thought forgiveness should look like. I began to contrast another's contrition against my standards and expectations rather than God's—then and only then would I forgive. But that moment never came, because my expectations of what true repentance and sorrow for wrongdoing should look like are faulty, wrong, and damaged. Unrealistic and unattainable. Therefore, I never ended up seeing what I wanted to see in my husband or my father because I didn't even know what I was looking for, nor did I grasp the truth that I shouldn't be looking in the first place. In my mind and by my standards, my dad and Jim never acted like they were sincerely sorry for what they did, so I didn't forgive them. Pride, the root of this night-mare, had sweet-talked me to place my own judgment above God's. It's outrageous and arrogant, but true—I set the standard. Who do I think I am? I don't know, because I don't see myself in light of His perfection, forgiveness, and grace. In light of His holiness, His moral purity, and His perfect love.

And so I continued to live (or die) with unforgiveness wrapped around my heart. The hurt was horrible, like a fresh, deep wound. This crushing pain lingered long and fierce. The demon of unforgiveness continued to torment me, dragging me down deep into an abyss of anger and bitterness. I knew this thing was trying to kill me. While I waited for unrealistic expectations to be fulfilled so I can forgive both of these men that I love, my heart struggled for freedom. Freedom from this evil that binds me. Buried six feet under this weight, my heart longed, even fought, to be freed from *myself* and the hurt I foolishly clung to.

Forgiveness will take me to this place where true freedom is found when I discover its Author. When I surrender all expectations and my

whole life to Him who creates life itself, what I've deeply longed for
from life's first breath will finally be found. And forgiveness will cover
my soul like the soothing balm that it is. First *for* me and then *through* me
extended to others; the ones God used to help teach me along the way—
the two prominent men in my life, my father and husband. But not yet.
At this point, there's much to learn, more living to be done, more growing. My heart still needs to be broken wide open so that, like stained
glass, it might be pieced back together in His image, allowing the light
of His love to shine through in all its beauty. This sinner still needs to
see and know that she needs and longs for a Savior.

◦—

"For all have sinned and fall short of the glory of God." He
smiles, beaming with wisdom. Joy-filled and contagious, my
uncle Mark continues, "While we were yet sinners, Jesus died
for us. We can't save ourselves. But He can and did, Jill."

Although I don't fully grasp why at the time, I know that
Uncle Mark's words are filled with wisdom that begins to heal
my broken heart. Every time he visits, he brings more of what
my soul craves.

Sin. Glory. Saved. Real love. What in the world is he talking
about? I don't understand, but I'm listening and hearing with
my heart because I need hope. I need something more and I
don't know where to find it. Although it's not clear to me why
or what, I crave what he has. And what I see in him is something more—more than Uncle Mark. It's bigger and beyond
what he alone can offer. Deep within, I know he has what I
need, what I've been longing for.

I try to understand and there's only one place I can think
of to begin...

So I take the Book in my hands and I find and read the

two verses he was talking about, Romans 3:23–24, "For all have sinned and fall short of the glory of God, and are justified freely by his grace through the redemption that came by Christ Jesus." I don't know where to find the other verse he mentioned, so I fumble through the thin, fragile pages, searching for freedom in the red and black letters. My eager eyes fall upon Romans 5:8, "But God demonstrates his own love for us in this: While we were still sinners, Christ died for us." Love? Death? I try to make sense out of what I'm reading—it's written in English but speaking to me in another language.

A language of the heart.

I find another page in the Book, a good page where I see the word "forgiveness" in bright lights. Underneath this word that is so much more than letters arranged on a page, it's life to me but I don't know this yet, I see more verses. More places to go and read with the hope of finding what the broken heart within me needs: to live, to love, and to forgive. If not for the trail of questions I begin to follow, I'd find myself almost dancing as I discover the incredible treasure tucked within these pages.

Ephesians 1:7–8, "In him we have redemption through his blood, the forgiveness of sins, in accordance with the riches of God's grace that he lavished on us with all wisdom and understanding."

Redemption. What does this mean? Blood—His, but why? Riches, grace, lavished. Beautiful words, but . . . Wisdom and understanding. How I deeply desire both! And so I ask . . . or pray, not fully understanding what it means to do either.

⌒

I had absolutely no idea what I was getting myself into the day I opened the Bible for the first time. While I assumed I was attempting to read it, I had no idea that its Author would read me. Without a full grip on the magnitude of the journey I was about to embark on, I dove in as deep as I could go. Like a mirror, this Book begins to reflect who I am and who God is and is not. He is not like us—not like you or me. For though we are made in His image, He is indescribable. Uncontainable. He opens His mouth and things unimaginable happen. He summons the stars by name and numbers the grains of sand on every seashore. He is the Author of life and breath, the Giver of each moment and all good things. What will I do with Him? With this treasure bound in worn black leather? What will become of little me in the shadow of the All-Consuming One? The truth of who this Father, King, Creator, Redeemer, Comforter, Keeper, Savior is overwhelms me and I begin to recognize and acknowledge my desperate need for Him. My pride is exposed for what it is—sin. An ugly, glaring, scarlet stain that has covered me.

But there are words in this Book that carry great and lasting promise, bringing with them the hope I ache for. "Come now, let us reason together," says the LORD. "Though your sins are like scarlet, they shall be as white as snow; though they are red as crimson, they shall be like wool" (Isa. 1:18). And so I come to Him. And I cry out, surrendering all that I am as my deep need becomes crystal clear—Jesus. The refiner's fire is burning away the impurities around my soul. I can actually feel the heavy burden lifting from within and I know that life has come to the barren landscape of my heart. He is healing the brokenhearted one and binding up her wounds. I find forgiveness and the rigid grip squeezing my heart begins to loosen. The weary and heavy-laden child that I am is finding rest for her soul through the love of the One who is gentle and humble in heart. Faith becomes my sight. I stop trying to hold myself up with my own jaded understanding and I begin to acknowledge and trust Him, the Unseen One, with all my heart, soul, mind, and strength. His thoughts are not my thoughts, neither are my ways His ways. I learn. I tremble at His Word and the beautiful way it's changing me. The mirror begins to reflect someone different, someone new, and I find myself beginning to look at my father and husband through the eyes of His heart, full of love and grace and forgiveness. I choose freedom and life, and I forgive . . . I am set free and life eternal begins—*now!* I look and find myself awestruck with wonder. I am no longer barren but walking through a lush, fragrant garden of hope.

∽

The house is quiet. Erin and Camryn are in school and Jim is out of town. Our Chihuahua Bella is snuggled in next to me as close as she can possibly get. With a fresh cup of hot coffee nearby, journal and Bible in hand, I'm ready for quiet time. Or so I think. I begin reading through the Bible study workbook lying across my lap. My pen is fast at work. As with most studies, I diligently fill in the answers to all the questions. Unfortunately, I'm a recovering perfectionist, so all the blanks must be filled in. My answers turn into paragraphs—ugh. And I come to these questions:

"Have you ever been betrayed?"

"What happened?"

"Where are you right now in the healing process?"

After reading the questions again, I stop and stare at each word, then look away to search for an answer. A bright-red cardinal darts by the picture window directly across from where I'm sitting. I glance back down at my workbook and read the questions again. My face twists into a perfect scowl at the thought of not being able to complete the discussion questions. I'm stumped. There's no answer to fill in the blanks. Nothing comes to me.

And then it hits me. I fall to the ground and fall apart. In a flood of tears swept deep into the heart of God by His overwhelming grace and love...

I had forgotten.

I was unable to fill in the blanks because, for the first time ever...

I had forgotten.

Miraculously, in that very moment, in the midst of a typical (or not so typical) Bible study question, God swept me off my feet and to my knees with His incredible forgiveness.

I realize for the very first time that I had truly forgiven...

And forgotten.

I had been betrayed.

I had been hurt to the very core of who I am.

I had struggled to forgive, bearing the burden of unforgiveness in my heart for years. I had persistently sought after the heart of God with the hope of finding the strength, grace, and wisdom to forgive. Sadly, unforgiveness had choked the life and love right out of me time and time again, tightening the grip of bitterness and hatred around my heart. It was horrible.

I thought I had forgiven and then another wave of disappointment and heartbreak would come crashing in and I would rehash the thing. Or maybe better put, the thing would rehash me! For so long I had wanted to run away from myself because I couldn't even stand me any longer. I longed to surrender, but I had no idea how to raise the white flag in my heart. At times I would even pray, "Lord, I don't know how to forgive the way You do, please help me—rescue me from unforgiveness. I want to forgive, but I can't do it without You, please HELP me." Some mornings I would ask God to help me forgive because I knew that even before I got out of bed I would need to surrender the anger trying to burrow its way into the depths of my heart. So as I sat there unable to fill in the blanks in my Bible study workbook, I was shocked. Overwhelmed. Thankful. Relieved. Free!

I had truly forgiven.

And only by the grace of God, I had forgotten.

And maybe I finally realized, to whatever extent I needed to in that moment, how very much God had forgiven me. "Her many sins have been forgiven—for she loved much. But he who has been forgiven little loves little"(Luke 7:47).

This was one of the most profound moments in my walk of faith thus far. I had forgotten the wrong that had been done. The moment when God brought me into the deep well of living water, revealing more to me than I could fathom and comprehend. Because He is God. He is love immeasurable. Because He forgives . . . and forgets.

> The LORD is compassionate and gracious, slow to anger, abounding in love. He will not always accuse, nor will he harbor his anger forever; he does not treat us as our sins deserve or repay us according to our iniquities. For as high as the heavens are above the earth, so great is his love for those who fear him; as far as the east is from the west, so far has he removed our transgressions from us. (Psalm 103:8–12)

~

Though not perfectly, I see more clearly. Now I seem to know in part, but someday I shall know fully, even as I am fully known. While I wait for the fullness of this knowing, a crown of beauty instead of ashes adorns my head. The oil of gladness and garments of praise and salvation cover me completely. A priceless treasure has been discovered in the midst of the rubble; love that is true, forgiveness that is real, deep, and eternal. My once-calloused heart is made new—softened and strengthened through grace. Forgiveness flows through the soul once hardened and without hope. Healing does come. I am forgiven and then...I forgive—and forget! And He loves through me, and I taste and see that the Lord really is good. This pain that caused my heart to break wide open is of the Lord. It is! It's the bridge to His heart. While the enemy of my soul wanted to use this unforgiveness to keep me trapped, God was orchestrating freedom in the middle of it all. Had I not been bent on protecting my heart with the shield of unforgiveness I would've never been exposed to my own need for forgiveness. Jesus filled in the blank on the page and exposed the darkness that was my heart. I look beyond the mirrored image into His heart and life imprinted upon mine. I find love through His forgiveness. And I love my father and husband afresh, a different kind of love that is beyond me. I love them more than I ever imagined possible—because He first loved me.

And even now, in the very moment that I write this, He tenderly speaks to me and ushers me into a deeper grace than I've known before.

"There's more healing to be found, Jill. You need to tell them that you're sorry."

I can't even move.

As I sit in stillness, the holiness of the moment moves me to tears.

Another apology is needed. My husband and father need to hear me say the liberating words..."I'm sorry." Out of my mouth my heart must speak, and I will seek forgiveness from them, for not extending it to them, for expecting so much from them, for allowing bitterness to divide what God has put together. Love overflows from a heart that God has pieced back together—my heart. And I'm filled with gratitude for the two men hand-picked by God for this incredible moment. An etching in time to show me how to live victoriously, love deeper, remember and never forget how amazing God is in the midst of it all. We will forgive yet again and somehow, miraculously, we will eventually forget. And believe it or not, through His love and by His grace . . .

You will too.

⌒

My heart is overflowing right now and I can hardly contain the joy because of the final moment I want to share with you. I hope this one rocks you like it did me.

I had just reviewed the final edited version of our family memoir *Without a Word* and I was spent. The writing and remembering had wiped me out emotionally, mentally, and physically. As I sat in my office pondering all that God had accomplished in my heart and through the writing, I was overcome and grateful. While looking out the window, a beautiful little sparrow swooped down and alighted on the deck railing right in front of me. In that tactile moment, I was reminded of the restoration and hope that had come to life through our heartbreak and pain.

Suddenly my melancholy musings were interrupted. "Hey, are you busy?" Jim asked, opening the door and peeking in.

"No, I was just thinking about all that has happened and the book and everything. What's up?" I queried.

"I need to tell you something. I talked to Erin," he said hesitantly.

There was a gentleness and humility about Jim that I had never witnessed before, causing my curiosity to spike. I immediately began to probe him for more information. "About what? What do you mean?" I asked.

"I realized that I needed to apologize to Erin. So I did." He sighed.

"For what? What happened?" I asked, staring quizzically into his dark-blue eyes. You know how it is when you want to know what's going on and the person with all the information isn't talking fast enough?

"I told Erin that I was sorry for all that I did to you. For not being faithful. I asked her to forgive me for not being the best husband and father I should have been and for hurting you the way I did."

Stunned and speechless, tears filled my eyes before I could get words out of my mouth. I couldn't believe what I'd just heard.

"What...How...When...What did she say? What did she do? Was she okay? Did she cry? How did you explain everything?" A barrage of questions came tumbling out of my mouth faster than I could articulate them.

"She was sitting on the couch in our room doing her homework. I just went in and told her I needed to talk to her. And then I just told her."

"Did she understand? What did she say?" I stammered, barely containing myself.

"She didn't say much, but she did say 'I forgive you, Daddy.'" Jim's eyes begin to water and he quickly changed the subject as he turned to make a run for it. But before he could get away, I hugged him tightly and whispered in his ear, "Thank you."

⸻

He didn't have to do this, but that's what happens when redemption is real and forgiveness is found through the love of Christ. That Love moves you to reach beyond yourself and do what's right regardless of the pain or inconvenience because you desire the highest good for others in spite of the cost. Love didn't just endure, it triumphed because of the joy set before Him, and that's what inspires those who know Him. Jim was free to seek forgiveness because he was secure and confident in the forgiveness he had received. Not only that, he now believed in it and was living beyond himself; revealing the love of God in a realistic, profound, and tangible way to his daughter.

Yes, Erin would have read the book. She would have found out for herself the despair God had rescued her parents from. But even so, Jim didn't have to ask her for forgiveness for something that he did to me. The truth is he didn't have to seek forgiveness from anyone. But he did. And because he humbled himself, God moved in his heart and reached through Jim to Erin. Ultimately it wasn't about Jim, Erin, or me, but about Christ and who He is in the midst of the moments like this that take our breath away.

I can't help but wonder what might have been if forgiveness had never been extended to Jim, to me, then to Erin. What if God didn't intervene? What if there were no rescue plan in place for us, for you, for all mankind? God didn't have to do what He did—He was never lacking anything and never had a need that only we could supply. No, God is fully content in and of Himself. He is complete. Yet He chose to love us, forgive us, and rescue us—to die instead of losing us forever and living without us. If He hadn't reached down into this mess we've made, there wouldn't be a greater story. Yes, there would be moments but they wouldn't amount to much. They'd be blowing in the wind like dead leaves in the sands of time—here today and gone tomorrow; a fleeting shadow, a vapor. Because that's what life is—a vapor, a dash between birth and death. And when all is said and done, what will your life amount to, really? Stick with me here because I'll bring this one home, I promise.

It adds up to a spiritual legacy that shapes both the character and destiny of the believer. As Jim humbled himself and asked forgiveness of Erin, he extended the love of Christ beyond his lifetime to the next generation. In that, Erin has her father's example to remember and call upon when she comes to her own crossroad of forgiveness. And my husband leaves a legacy in his daughter and through the life he lived, that when his time has passed and he joins Hunter in heaven, his life will still speak.

⌒

You know, I'm just wondering, have you noticed that I've left something out? There's something about forgiveness that we need to talk about. It's kind of like the proverbial "elephant in the room," one of those things we'd rather just ignore or get to at another time—like never. But we're not going to do that. We're going to talk about it, deal with it, and be done with it. I hope that sounds like a good idea to you.

So what about forgiving your enemy? We've all been there, and most of us are there right now in one way or another—dragging around that nasty burden that continues to get heavier and heavier every day. Truth is, that thing will continue to press in and weigh you down like a ball and chain until you deal with it—whatever "it" is. We live in a desperately broken and deeply fallen world, so I can only imagine what your "it" might be. It doesn't really matter what it is, because at the end of the day (or right this minute) you *need* to forgive. You may not even *want* to, but forgiveness is more of a life-and-death issue than most of us realize—it's a *need* whether it's a *want* or not!

Maybe you feel justified by your attitude and unforgiveness because you've been hurt so badly. Maybe you feel it's wrong or don't even know how to forgive if someone isn't sorry and doesn't ask to be forgiven…I hear you. Because of the injustices we suffer we often feel entitled to our hardened hearts because the simple truth is, what happened to us is not right—but neither are the things we've done to others, even if we've never been caught or seen. God sees. And when any of those He loves (meaning everybody) gets hurt—He hurts. It comes out of His hide just as parents hurt when their child is wounded or slighted. As if we have the right to think, feel, and act the way we do because we've earned it—we've paid for it with our pain. The worst part about carrying on like this is that our unforgiveness begins to blind us to our own shortcomings and wrongdoings, shrouding our hearts and shutting out the light of hope. It was Heartbreak 101 for me, and I aced the course without breaking a sweat, dying a little more each day!

An unforgiving spirit is a harsh taskmaster with no reservations about cracking the whip and leaving deep wounds infected with self-pity, pride, and anger that simmer beneath the surface of your life. The net effect is that it shapes our relationships, because we relate to others through our wounding and the resulting mistrust. It doesn't just hurt, it damages us—changes who we are and often the direction our lives take.

But consider Jesus, our example. Hebrews 12:2 explains that Jesus endured the cross for the joy set before Him. Everything He suffered was worth it because of the bottom line—He reconciled the people He loved so dearly, ransoming them from the oppression of their sin. It was such a joyous prospect that it made the terror of the cross worth enduring. Can you even imagine? Because He wanted to save you and me (even in our sin—when we were *enemies* of God). He endured the cross. It's so ridiculous and radical. Outrageous! But He did it so we would find in Him (and only through Him) the ability to do the same.

Once God's forgiveness begins to soften your raw and unrefined soul, causing you to see how much you've been forgiven, it changes you. It not only moves you to forgive, but creates a passion to do so. Because you're free! And just as God longs to freely forgive all His beloved children, even those who will never seek Him, He can now peer into your soul and see that same image! I've been refined and unforgiveness has been purified from my life. And you know what? Everything I went through in order to bring me to this very moment was worth the freedom God graciously gave me through understanding and experiencing His forgiveness.

He longs for us to be free and He did everything necessary for us to experience true freedom. This isn't easy, and please forgive me if I've made it appear to be so. No, it's not easy—it took a cross and a perfect Savior to make it happen. But it happened. He did it for you and me so that we would no longer have to drag that ball and chain that He took care of. It's finished. Receive this...He is *for* you. He will help you right where you are, in the midst of this journey, to snap those chains of unforgiveness. Don't let another day—another minute—go by. Forgive!

What to Remember and Never Forget...

- Unforgiveness will wrap itself around your heart like a vise, causing you to die a little more on the inside each day. A forgiving attitude, however, is absolutely liberating and it will bring life to your withered soul.
- The deeper the darkness, the brighter the light shines. And though you may think you're hiding from your hurt in the darkness of the lies you buy into, you're really running from the light of truth. No worries, though, His loving arms are open and ready to set you free.
- Harboring an unforgiving heart is every bit as sinful as the very sin you won't forgive in the first place. It is sheer bondage in an attempt to be free of the hurt you feel.
- You may think you're protecting your heart behind this barrier of unforgiveness, but what you're really doing is hiding in a cage in which you trap yourself. Yet, though the enemy hopes to use your unforgiveness against you to keep you trapped, God will guide you to freedom through it all.

Prayer...

> *My precious Savior, you've saved me from myself, and if I'm not saved from that I'm not saved from anything—*

thank you so much, from the very bottom of my heart. I am both humbled and hopeful at the extent of your forgiveness, there is truly no sin I have committed or will commit that is greater than your love; no darkness that its light cannot pierce. Help me to walk in this same spirit and attitude, with your vulnerability and strength toward all those who have and will hurt me, that I might show my love and gratitude to you. And above all, help me show the world Jesus.

Truths about Forgiveness to Etch Upon Your Heart:

But you are a forgiving God, gracious and compassionate, slow to anger and abounding in love. (Nehemiah 9:17)

Praise the LORD, my soul, and forget not all his benefits—who forgives all your sins and heals all your diseases, who redeems your life from the pit and crowns you with love and compassion, who satisfies your desires with good things so that your youth is renewed like the eagle's. (Psalm 103:2–7)

If you, LORD, kept a record of sins, Lord, who could stand? But with you there is forgiveness, so that we can, with reverence, serve you. (Psalm 130:3–4)

For he has rescued us from the dominion of darkness and brought us into the kingdom of the Son he loves, in whom we have redemption, the forgiveness of sins. (Colossians 1:13–14)

Bear with each other and forgive one another if any of you has a grievance against someone. Forgive as the Lord forgave you. (Colossians 3:13)

If we confess our sins, he is faithful and just and will forgive us our sins and purify us from all unrighteousness. (1 John 1:9)

chapter four

suffering

Our Lord did not change His world so much through His miracles as He did through His suffering.

Cardinal O'Connor

$\mathcal{G}$randma, it's okay." I grab her wrinkled, sun-spotted hand and try to stop it from shaking. I desperately want to console her.

"Okay, honey," she responds with a gentle smile as tears stream down her face. Her eyes look right past me. What is she looking at? I wonder. Over my shoulder the waves ripple gently along the shore. The ocean is still and quiet.

Grandma loves the beach. Before she got sick she used to collect seashells. It was an extra-special Christmas if Grandma Jean made you an animal out of her seashell collection. She made me a mama duck and two babies one year. What a treasure.

I ponder these things in my heart while I sit with her on the beach.

Her bottom lip continues to quiver and she cries. For no reason, but maybe for all the obvious reasons, she sits there with a blank stare while tears continue to fall, one right after the other.

For the first time in all the years that we have watched her slowly drift away, it hits me—she's dying and there's nothing anyone can do about it. Every day we see less and less of her and more of this grotesque disease. Why does this have to happen? Why can't we do something to help her? Isn't there any sort of medication she can take to make this go away?

The doctors say she has Alzheimer's and dementia and they've done all they can to help her. It's just a matter of time, and it's breaking Grandpa Jack's heart. It breaks all of our hearts. The Grandma Jean we know and love is still in that sick body. She still wants to play No-Peek Greek cards—and beat us. She's unashamedly competitive and smart; she knows how to play her cards. But this hand she's been dealt, this disease she must fight and wrestle with...it's fierce. She has a very difficult time remembering things, like who her grandchildren are, and it makes her cry a lot. This dreadful disease keeps her from the simple pleasures in life, like making her famous tea ring that her ten children and twenty-plus grandchildren love. I miss her goofy faces and funny jokes. I miss her. And sometimes I miss her the most when I'm sitting right next to her.

This beautiful and dreadfully sad moment on the beach with Grandma Jean breaks me. Will this be the last time I get to hold her hand, touch her warm skin?

Throughout most of my childhood I had not experienced suffering. I remember the day my great-grandma Emma (Grandma Jean's mother) died and the pain I felt as I watched my family endure her funeral with such deep sorrow. Still, I had never witnessed Great-Grandma Emma actually suffering. I never watched her physically endure sickness or disease. What I remember most vividly is her loving touch, beautiful smile, and delicious lemon meringue pies. So other than the typical struggles that most of us experience my childhood was blessedly shielded from real suffering, and I knew very little about it.

But then, as one year drifted into the next, I found myself much older and my grandma Jean very sick.

Grandma Jean was just as much a friend to me as she was a grandmother. I loved and adored her, and when I heard that she was not well, I just couldn't believe it. She's tough, I thought. I know she'll rise above this challenge and come out stronger as a result of it. But that's not what happened; instead she suffered until her last breath. I pondered this and tried to make sense of it all, because that's what we do. We try to wrap our hearts and minds around things that are impossible to understand. It's self-preservation—a way of reinforcing the ramparts around our comfort zones and trying to somehow control what we have no control over. And in doing so, we conjure up pocket-sized, synthetic solutions to vast, God-sized circumstances. Worse than that, we try to mold and shape God into what we think He should look and act like—resulting in a god of our making rather than the One who IS. So we, the small and powerless, craft an almighty god in our own feeble image and direct him to solve the problems that overwhelm us in the way we, in the smallness of our vision, deem best! Of course, since *we* fashioned this god, we are greater than it is, making us . . . well, enough said!

～

"Hasn't he suffered enough?" I cry out to God. "Why are You letting this happen to him? Why won't you do something? Let me suffer instead. This is too much for him. Please stop this. Please rescue my Hunterboy. What has he done to deserve this?"

The more I cry out in frustration and anguish, the weaker I feel. I'm balled up on the floor in my closet. Exasperated. Exhausted and confused, I squeeze my Bible against my chest as tightly as possible. My body rocks back and forth, writhing in anguish as tears stream uncontrollably down my cheeks.

I stop and grab the journal and pen lying next to me on the floor. And I carve these words as big as the page space, ripping paper as I write. "HELP ME! I HATE THIS! I CAN'T DO THIS ANYMORE! TAKE THIS CUP OF SUFFERING AWAY FROM HIM! PLEASE! RIGHT NOW. DO SOMETHING!"

We've tried everything to help Hunter. He's been on almost every medicine and machine known to man.

Why are you sitting here feeling sorry for yourself? Hunter's the one suffering. Get up! Crazy, irrational thoughts bombard my mind.

I need to pull myself together. Hunter needs me. I whisper and try to encourage myself so I can get up off the floor and out of this miserable funk. I'm desperate for help. I know this. I need strength that is beyond me. Power made perfect in my weakness, because Hunterboy needs me.

And in the uneasy hush of my closet, I rip a sweatshirt down from the closest shelf, burying my face in it. Feeling like I'm riding an avalanche, I scream as loud as I can, for none but my clothes to hear, and shatter the stillness with a thousand jagged tears.

Suffering. The real face of physical suffering was a stranger—unrecognizable to me until my one and only son, Hunter, was diagnosed with the disease that eventually took his life. Although I had watched others struggle, nothing I ever experienced could compare to what I witnessed day after day for the eight and a half years of his life. I wrestled with God about suffering for as long as Hunter was alive, and I still do every once in a while. But that's okay, because He knows me and loves me whether I'm plagued with doubts and questions or a pillar of faith and confidence. He remains faithful to me even in those moments when my faith falters. At times I couldn't see beyond the murky veil of our circumstances. They were so intense and the stifling heat of the fiery trials we endured confounded me as I struggled to grasp their meaning and resolution. Where was the love of God in this nightmare I could not awaken from? Ultimately, I wrestled with things incomprehensible apart from His revealing, and my mind constantly played tricks on me as I did. I often felt smothered as the distortion of what appeared to be true tried to choke my fragile, budding faith.

But while circumstances may have mocked my hopes, I knew there was more beyond their veil. So I'd spend hours devouring God's Word while I cared for Hunter in the lonely midnight hours. The life I watched my son endure forced me to my knees and kept me there, making the truth of who God says He is more and more real to me. And in the throes of this battle, my heart and mind fought to believe, torn between truth and lies.

With my son's suffering and all that I didn't understand, I ran to Christ and His suffering and all that He did for me and for Hunter. I learned that it's okay to long for the cup to pass and even beg for it to because Jesus Himself asked His Father if there was any other way. Only after He went through it, enduring the cross and scorning its shame, would the reality of the greater joy come, the redemption and salvation of mankind. Jesus carried the burden and paid the penalty we owed but could never pay even with our greatest efforts—His love bridged the gap from God's heart to ours. In my search for understanding I found that because Jesus' suffering was (and is) redemptive, God is redeeming something through our suffering. No tear is ever wasted. What God has allowed, no matter how painful, He will redeem for His glory and our highest good.

Because of the cross and all that Jesus accomplished there, my son's suffering has purpose, meaning, and even hope. And your suffering does too—it's not arbitrary or in vain. We can run to the cross with all of our suffering and pour our broken hearts out there because of Jesus' suffering. The beauty of what Jesus did that day on Calvary makes the suffering that we must endure beautiful too. That might sound ridiculous and crazy, especially coming from a mother who watched her son suffer every day for over eight years. I know. But God's ways and thoughts are higher than our ways and thoughts (see Isa. 55:8). He allowed His One and Only Son, Jesus, to suffer—a suffering beyond anything our earthly minds and hearts can fathom. Love died so we might actually live. But more, Love was crucified so we might have an unshakable fortress to run into with all that we don't understand in this life. A shelter and harbor of hope when the storm waves try to drag us under and into their darkened depths. A place where the Man of Sorrows, acquainted with grief, waits, risen with arms wide open for the gathering of your tears.

God's apparent or perceived inactivity in the midst of our suffering doesn't mean that He has abandoned or forsaken us—that He doesn't care. In fact, it's when we are buried deep under the weight of our trials that He is actively involved, doing His greatest work. We don't always sense His presence, but He is there. We want answers, but our questions enrich us even more, for they drive us to the surpassing gift of more of Him.

It took everything within me to share my testimony that day. The women's event had been on my calendar for a long time, but how could I have known that I would be asked to endure the unendurable? Absolutely drained, I came into the event at an energy deficit because I was unable to get enough sleep the previous night. I was bone tired, road weary, and, as unspiritual as it sounds, I just wanted to share and get home to the kids as fast as I could. While my mother took care of details and finalized logistics with the event coordinator, I took advantage of the rare alone time to sit in the car and pray. It was a tough night—I felt less gifted and more inadequate than ever as I curled up with God in my four-wheel-drive prayer closet.

"Lord, I have nothing to give these women. I don't want to go in there. I can't go in. Please intervene. Please fill me with Your life, Your hope, and Your presence. I'm so tired. I don't want to be here. You know how I feel right now. You know my every thought. I will do this in Your strength alone. I can't share our story unless You go before me. You know every person in that building intimately. You know why they're here today. You know what they need to hear. Please speak through me. Please touch hearts and lives like only You can . . ."

The flesh and the spirit struggled a little longer, contending for my heart and mind, but I was confident that the will of God would somehow carry the day in spite of me as I slipped quietly from the truck. Walking over to the building where hundreds of women were gathered, I thought about the strangers I would meet. All of them with a story of their own. Each story significant and precious to God.

What do I have to offer these women—but Jesus? I have nothing to give. I need a Savior as much as they do, my soul thirsts for living water just as theirs does.

After a beautiful worship experience with a room full of hearts united before God, I shared my testimony. Upon finishing, a line of women formed to greet me near the podium; God had miraculously touched many. Some had eyes overflowing with tears, while others were anxious to talk, sensing our kindred spirits and wanting more.

As the line dwindled and the last few women made their way toward me, a pair of eyes etched with deep abiding sorrow met mine. Her careworn face was carved with grief, it was obvious that she tried her best to pull herself together. She was patient enough to wait to talk to me, and somehow before she uttered a word I knew her story would wreck me—and it did.

After we greeted each other with a firm hug, she poured out her life, her story of loss, unrivaled heartbreak, and devastating anguish.

She had lost three children. One, a teenager, succumbed to leukemia. Another, in her twenties, had died in a car accident. The third child had committed suicide, unable to cope with the deaths of the other two.

Stunned, I stood there in shock as she continued to pour out her broken heart to me, and thought to myself, What in the world am I going to say to this woman? The story of Job is standing right in front of me. Maybe I should say nothing and just hug her?

Overwhelmed by her story, I was completely floored. Before she walked away, I asked her if we could pray together, yet as the words left my mouth, I felt completely inadequate to even pray. Who was I to say a single word to petition God in the face of a heartbreak that eclipsed anything I could imagine? She had suffered so much—and survived it all.

"I know where my children are right now," she said firmly. "They all knew the Lord. I'm confident that I will see them again. I'm so thankful they knew Jesus." Still stunned, we prayed and then hugged good-bye, and I watched in awe as she walked away with her friend.

As I gathered my things, I heard my heart whisper over and over, "There's no way I could ever handle that. There's just no way. God, what in the world was that? Why? How did she survive—much less triumph—with her faith intact and praise in her heart?"

Of course I knew the answer to my question—Jesus was and is her survival, her triumph, the strength of her heart. Period. She was still living and breathing after the death of three children because she was being held in the strong hands of God. As you can imagine, I'll never forget this moment.

I've had the privilege of meeting hundreds of precious women through the opportunities that God has given me to share throughout the country. Many times I'm able to talk with them and find my way between the lines of the many stories that converge at such an event. It is rarely anything but deep to search the joys and sorrows, fears and faith, hopes and nuances of the destinies that merge while I open my heart from a pulpit.

Believe it or not, I've met women buried under even more anguish over the lives of their children than that precious sister whose three children had passed away. I'm talking about women with kids who by all outward appearances are thriving and living well, yet they are dying inside because they're separated from Life—from God. I've peered through eyes flooded with waves of pain, into the hearts beneath that suffer in desperation for the salvation of an only child gone astray.

The woman in the moment I shared above suffered a loss that was beyond comprehension—I wouldn't dare try to say I understand, even though my own loss bears some similarity. I could only weep with her.

Yet I have met other mothers, whose children have wandered far from the truth, only to drift aimlessly through a wilderness of sin and shame. These women lament an even greater loss, their hope balanced precariously on a razor's edge. How can this be? How can the ache in a mother's soul for the life of a lost child appear to be just as strong as the depth of a woman's loss of three children?

While it can sound like a spiritual spin job, it is a reality and it plays no favorites, takes no prisoners, and knows no compromise: the greatest suffering we will ever know and experience is separation from God.

My friend (the woman who lost three children—I call her friend because that's what I consider her to be now that we've shared our hearts) knew the light of Christ's love; the salvation He purchased for her and her children with His very life. Her pain was real, and yet her hope in the eternal made it possible for her to press on with hope and purpose, because she knew that she would see her three children again someday in heaven. In stark contrast, the mothers I've met whose children are trying to fill their empty souls with earthly pursuits and passing treasures watch helplessly as their kids are sucked into a world of darkness and eternal separation from the only One who can save them. Their pain is crushing because they realize that there is no hope unless Jesus intervenes. It is a relentless sequence of pain, sorrow, and suffering.

We're all lost.

We're all separated from God.

We all wander through deep darkness...

Until Jesus intervenes!

I don't know what you're going through right now. But I know with all of my heart that God loves *you* and that through His Son, Jesus, He made a way for you, a place for you to run to with all that you're going through right now. God uses the deep losses and sorrows in all of our lives to move us closer to the Man of Sorrows. In fact, I believe our suffering actually moves us into the very depths of the heart of God. I love how J. I. Packer explains what I'm trying to say. "Perhaps His purpose is simply to draw us closer to Himself in conscious communion with Him; for it is often the case, as all the saints know, that fellowship with the Father and Son is most vivid and sweet, and Christian joy is greatest, when the cross is the heaviest."[1]

Some of what I've shared here might contradict what you've been taught or what you believe to be true about suffering. I'm not a theologian nor do I claim to know and understand all there is to know about suffering, God, and His Word. What I share here is based first and foremost on what I've experienced in my life and walk with the Lord thus far as supported by Scripture. Certainly I have a lot more to learn and hopefully a lot more living to do.

As graciously as I know how, I have tried to share what suffering has meant to me while enduring it. How it has devastated me, changed me, and yet ultimately enriched my life. My joy truly has been the greatest when my cross was the heaviest, and I'm absolutely convinced it can be the same for you. My dear friend Katie (I share a story about her in a later chapter) once said, "Suffering really is a gift—it makes you heaven-hungry." She's right. Suffering takes our focus off the temporal and irrelevant. It moves us to look beyond the veil of our circumstances into the heart of God and the great hope of heaven. Suffering also reminds us that life is not predictable and very seldom goes according to how we had hoped and planned. What we believe about God and His character will determine how we endure in the midst of our trials. If we trust that God is in control, working out the details of our lives and that nothing can thwart His perfect plan for us—then we can look beyond our circumstances to the hope that Christ alone graciously provides. His resurrection gave us a forever hope beyond the here and now—and how we understand and receive this hope alters the way we live life (including suffering) right now—in this moment.

Everything we experience—every tragedy, tear, joy, and celebration—doesn't happen arbitrarily, it is subject to the sovereignty of God. If He allows you to walk through the Valley of the Shadow of Death, it's because of love—even though it may appear otherwise. He loves you. He loves you enough to *not* take the cup of suffering from you. That's because He sees the greater glory, the other side of the heartbreak. Remember, He watches from eternity and contrasts our circumstances against our eternal well-being.

Just as He did not remove the cup of suffering from His One and Only Son, He will not take the cup from you either. It's for your good and His glory; otherwise you would not have to experience the trial. I know, I'm thinking of that moment with the woman and the death of her three children too. I don't understand it all. I don't know how she could stand there, much less share her story. There's no answer—but God. Because it's beyond us; beyond our ability to grasp. This seems to make no sense and contradicts the natural way we look at life. Exactly!

But we need to remember, although it's incredibly hard to do most of the time, God is not like us. We try desperately to mold Him into our image, to make Him act and be like we think He should. We think that we would do things differently, better, and yet we see only the moment. We don't know what the next minute—much less the future—holds, particularly beyond the end of time. But He does—He's God, and He holds the future and forever. If He has allowed suffering to shatter life as you know it, He must have something great He wants to accomplish in and through you. I wish I could delete that previous sentence because in a way it comes off kind of trite.

But is it? If God is God, where else are we going to go? Who else can we go to with our questions, fears, and doubts? If He's God and He has allowed suffering in all its forms to invade your life, it all has purpose. And maybe that's where healing actually begins, in believing and trusting that God is God despite all that you're going through.

Your tears are not in vain. He sees you and knows exactly what you need at all times. He is your greatest need, and if suffering is the path to seeing Him more clearly and knowing Him in a deeper way—He will allow it.

Honestly, it's almost an outrageous thing to say, characterizing suffering in redemptive and creative terms. It is more than a ten-minute conversation or chapter in a book—even more than a whole book. You can't superficially wrap historical savagery like the Holocaust in spirituality, any more than you can reduce heartbreak to religious explanations. Still, the problem of pain and suffering is nothing new, and many have written insightfully and sensitively on the topic.

In fact, legendary Christian apologist and writer C. S. Lewis wrote a fantastic book on it with that very title: *The Problem of Pain*. And it's a real problem for some of us who believe in an all-powerful God of love. The conflict is sort of obvious, don't you think? If God is all loving and all powerful, then His love would engage His power to end suffering and pain—right? If suffering, which appears to be inconsistent with love, continues, then some wonder if maybe He doesn't have all power. I mean, when Hunter was suffering, if I could have stopped it of course I would have, even if it cost me my life!

⌒

There's another characteristic of suffering that may be even more difficult to grasp, but it's as intense and powerful as anything we've shared thus far. It's the way suffering reveals what's real. I find this to be true on many levels. Take Jesus for an example. The sinfulness of man was revealed in His suffering—just look at the hatred, pride, selfishness, anger, and on it goes, all expressed in the way He was framed, beaten beyond recognition, and nailed to the cross.

When we suffer, we cannot fake it. It's a little hard to pretend to be something you're not when circumstances "squeeze" you. Like a tube of toothpaste, when we're squeezed, what's inside comes out. If we're filled with the grace of God, then tough situations bring out that grace. But if our graciousness is more spiritual adornment than spiritual reality, we won't stack up to the circumstances, and what's really there will rear its head.

I don't fully understand what the Bible means when it says "because he who has suffered in his body is done with sin" (1 Pet. 4:1), but I have to believe there is a connect to this idea that suffering reveals what is real. What this verse is plainly saying is that when you suffer, you do not sin—no pretense, posturing, pride, nothing but sheer reality—it's all you! And maybe that is one of the silver linings in suffering, a pure heart that cries to God with no confidence in our talents or abilities, our spirituality or command of Scripture. Just a broken heart before God, the sort of heart that draws His attention (see Ps. 51:17 and 34:18) and moves Him to action.

I need to share one more moment with you that I think will bring this chapter to a perfect close. It's time to get writing. I'm days away from the deadline for handing in a draft of this manuscript. It's been a crazy week. Both Erin and Camryn have had basketball games every night. Jim left this morning for the Super Bowl in Indianapolis. There's so much to do and I'm getting overwhelmed to say the least. After dropping the girls off at school, I get home, grab another cup of coffee, and head into the office for some quiet time and writing. Papers are strewn everywhere; evidence that I've been writing and rewriting. I clear the area around my keyboard and accidentally awaken my computer from its overnight slumber. My home screen displays a document that's not mine, so of course I have to find out what it is. And this is what I start reading:

> No words can describe what it feels like to watch those closest to you suffer every day of their life. My brother, Hunter, was born with and then diagnosed with a fatal neurological disease called Krabbe when he was four months old. We were told that he would not live to see his second birthday. We watched Hunter deteriorate, and

for a time we treated him as though he were dying, but when Jesus intervened everything changed. We started treating Hunter like he was living, because he was! It was not until we realized that we were all spiritually dead that we started living. I was five years old when I accepted Jesus into my life. I prayed the prayer of salvation with my grandma and Hunter on a night I will never forget. Watching Hunter suffer is indescribable. He was not only my brother but also my best friend. It was Hunter's suffering that led me to Jesus' suffering. Sometimes I wonder how something so painful could lead me to something so beautiful. Though Hunter's suffering was unbearably ugly, somehow it was beautiful because through his pain I saw all the pain that Jesus took on my behalf. Hunter went to heaven on August 5, 2005, at the age of eight. Though it has been six years, every day seems like an uphill battle. Every day is still a struggle because I miss him more than words can describe. Even through the trials and even through the pain I am continuing to grow in my relationship with Christ. It is because of someone who spoke volumes without saying a word. This little boy who never spoke a single word changed my life.

⌒

I'm groping for words right now, reaching for a way to communicate what's overflowing from my heart. This cry of Erin's tender, broken heart is not something that would fall from the pen of a typical sixteen-year-old. This type of reasoning and maturity is not of this world, but rings of the eternal, the heavenly. It is a perfect picture of what happens when your home, values, and way of life are not rooted in time, but in the everlasting Kingdom of Love. Rooted where forgiveness and redemption change everything because a Hero—a King with nail-scarred hands—has rescued His heartbroken little princess. And in the rescuing, He made the suffering that hurt so deeply the very path of deliverance she needed.

Even after Erin's beautiful testimony, you may not be able to reconcile an all-powerful God of love with suffering—and that's okay. Because even in your doubt and unbelief, He loves you. And maybe you don't have to even try to figure this all out. Maybe it's enough that God knows how to reconcile this paradox. Maybe it's enough that we know…

God knows.

What to Remember and Never Forget…

- Suffering is common to all mankind. Everyone will face painful trials—no one is exempt.
- Suffering is part of God's plan for His children.
- The cross of Christ is where we find hope and meaning for the suffering we experience.
- God will redeem our tears, allowing light and life to flow out of suffering and darkness.
- God wants to comfort you in the midst of your trials. And with the comfort He gives you, you are to comfort others when they go through difficult times.

Prayer…

> *Dear God, I don't fully understand how suffering has a redemptive quality, but I know you do—for You suffered more than any man throughout history's tear-stained pages. I trust in Your love for me, and I get that eternal values govern Your decision. Lord, help them govern mine as well—I live far too much in time. Help me drink deeply*

from every cup You offer me, knowing it is ultimately filled with Your selfless love for me and passion for my highest good that I might know You, not just know about You. Help me to believe in Your love though circumstances may try to tell me it's not real, and by Your grace, love You when it's hard and costly, just as You love me.

Truths about Suffering to Etch Upon Your Heart:

Those who sow in tears will reap with songs of joy. (Psalm 126:5)

Not only so, but we also rejoice in our sufferings, because we know that suffering produces perseverance; perseverance, character; and character, hope. And hope does not disappoint us, because God has poured out his love into our hearts by the Holy Spirit, whom he has given us. (Romans 5:3–5)

Praise be to the God and Father of our Lord Jesus Christ, the Father of compassion and the God of all comfort, who comforts us in all our troubles, so that we can comfort those in any trouble with the comfort we ourselves have received from God. For just as the sufferings of Christ flow into our lives, so also through Christ our comfort overflows. If we are distressed, it is for your comfort and salvation; if we are comforted, it is for your comfort, which produces in you patient endurance of the same sufferings we suffer. And our hope for you is firm, because we know that just as you share in our sufferings, so also you share in our comfort. (2 Corinthians 1:3–7)

For it has been granted to you on behalf of Christ not only to believe on him, but also to suffer for him. (Philippians 1:29)

Consider it pure joy, my brothers, whenever you face trials of many kinds, because you know that the testing of your faith develops perseverance. Perseverance must finish its work so that you may be mature and complete, not lacking anything. (James 1:2–4)

In this you greatly rejoice, though now for a little while you may have had to suffer grief in all kinds of trials. These have come so that your faith—of greater worth than gold, which perishes even though refined by fire—may be proved genuine and may result in praise, glory and honor when Jesus Christ is revealed. (1 Peter 1:6–7)

And the God of all grace, who called you to his eternal glory in Christ, after you have suffered a little while, will himself restore you and make you strong, firm and steadfast. To him be the power for ever and ever. Amen. (1 Peter 5:10–11)

chapter five

giving

*Each man should give what he has decided
in his heart to give, not reluctantly or under
compulsion, for God loves a cheerful giver.*
$\qquad\qquad\qquad\qquad\qquad$ *2 Corinthians 9:7*

$\mathcal{L}$ooking out the window, I'm waiting and watching. A maroon Chevy Cavalier rumbles by, splashing black slush all over the place; its muffler must have fallen off because the noise is loud and obnoxious. But for a moment, the unwanted sound distracts me from waiting and watching.

"Where is she?" I whisper to myself and to the snowflakes softly drifting out the picture window. My body is pressed up against the glass, close enough that my cheeks blush and feel the chill in the air. It's winter and she's not home yet. My younger brother, Jack, provides a much needed interruption as he bounces into the room.

"What are you doing?" he chimes into my silence.

"I'm watching for Mom," I respond with frustration.

He wiggles in next to me close to the glass and we both impatiently wait . . .

And watch.

The breath from our lungs almost shakes the glass as we exhale, and Jack draws pictures of animals on the fogged-up window. I know he's waiting and watching too. Breathing all over the entire window becomes a game to us now and a blessed distraction that suppresses our worry. I write my name in big capital letters, J-I-L-L, and start to trace my fingers in the shape of a heart. A bolt of light breaks into our fun, filling our drawings with life and our hearts with joy.

"She's home." We both erupt with excitement and relief as we leave our window masterpieces and race to the front door.

"Mom, why are you home so late?" I probe.

"Well, I did Meals on Wheels today after work. So how was your day?" she responds as she walks a little wearily toward the kitchen table.

My brother and I follow behind her like little ducklings.

"Who's ready for some dinner?" she says with excitement.

"I'm starving!" Jack shouts as he sits down at the table.

"What did the people eat that you gave food to?" I ask with wonder.

❧

I've been watching my mother for as long as I can remember. She was just eighteen and fresh out of high school when she had me. My parents were trying to make ends meet and raise my brother, Jack, and me while they were still growing up themselves, for heaven's sake. And yet she was always giving of herself; her time, her money—which was barely enough for our family to get by—her affection, and her whole heart.

I often wondered why she did the things she did. Like why did she go and do Meals on Wheels after a long day at work? Wasn't she tired? Didn't she just want to come home? In a way, I suppose I was sort of jealous; selfishly wanting more of her for myself—the part she so graciously gave away to others, to strangers she didn't even know.

⌒

"I'm starving," Jack says as he throws his duffel bag and climbs into the backseat of the car.

I roll my eyes and murmur, "Ugh. He's always hungry."

A day of school for my brother and me, followed by football and cheerleading practice. The rumble of teenage tummies is loud enough for Mom to hear. She's a good cook. But just the thought of the twenty-minute drive home on top of all the time it's going to take for her to whip up one of her delicious casseroles (or anything else, for that matter), makes our bellies growl even louder. The drive to pick us up after a stress-laden day at work is long. Her eyes are joy-filled yet dull with weariness. She has worked so hard to be a mom while climbing the corporate ladder of worldly success. She's intelligent and beautiful. I love her and want to be more like her.

"So how about we stop at McDonald's tonight?"

Mother's words reach our ears and we erupt with excitement. This is a treat for us. My parents work hard. Money doesn't grow on the tree in the backyard. Every month it's a struggle to pay the mortgage, electric, and water bill, to make ends meet. I hear my parents argue about money often, so we appreciate this welcome dinner surprise.

"Sweet! I'm getting a fish sandwich with..."

"A hamburger with..." Jack interrupts my order.

"Relax."

We all order.

As we approach the window to pay, my mother digs into her purse for money.

"I'd like to pay for the person behind us," she says to the worker.

Immediately I turn toward the backseat just as Jack turns to look out the back window. We're both wildly curious.

The aroma of McDonald's french fries fills the car as my mother hands me the bag of food to disperse.

"Mom, who was in the car behind us and why did you pay for them?" I exclaim with confusion as I dig into our bag.

"Yeah," Jack adds while reaching into the front seat for food.

"I don't know who's in the car," she responds. "I just thought they might need me to buy them dinner tonight." Her eyes are full of grace.

"But we don't have enough money to buy food for people!" A confused and frustrated teenage girl belts out these words. I really would like a pair of clogs or new jeans. My selfish wants and desires are weighing this act of giving for value and worth. Are the strangers worth this gift? She doesn't even know them.

Jack's already eating and doesn't say anything.

We're quiet as we all fill our hungry tummies, but my heart and mind stir as I ponder this giving. We need the money, so why does she give like this? I wonder silently. How do you even know if the receiver is thankful for this unexpected gift? It's McDonald's.

I can still remember and visualize—even smell the fries—that moment at the McDonald's drive-thru that afternoon. Confused, I didn't understand the gift and grace of giving like my mother did—I didn't get human need because my experience with it was so limited, my mom and dad made sure of that! I was an immature, selfish teenager; focused on all that this world was supposed to give me rather than what I might dare to give back.

My mother challenged me more by the way she lived than anything else, making me think much more deeply than I wanted to. She gave and gave—to total strangers, and in my youthful ignorance, I just didn't understand it. The money she spent that we didn't really have could have been used to buy something better. Maybe for me! Yet, in the throes of my teenaged contradictions, I found myself wanting to be more like her. Maybe it wasn't about the money at all? Could it really be as simple and profound as a heart that reaches outside of itself, choosing to give rather than take? Choosing selflessness over selfishness? Choosing to be the difference over the status quo?

She didn't just care about her family, she cared about people, even strangers, people she may never know, didn't owe a thing, and would never cross paths with again because that's who she is. Her compassion spread to everyone whose life she touched; they all got caught in her gravitational field, whether she was meeting their needs or praying for them. People noticed her smile and were drawn to the passion and joy that radiated from her. This isn't just a trait a grateful daughter saw in a wonderful mother, it was obvious to everyone who knew her. And as strange as it may be in these self-absorbed times, people who don't even know her *still* sense the way she sincerely cares about them when their lives touch. They see that she's different.

"There must be a mistake," Mother proclaimed with confidence. "I don't believe it. There has to be something we can do. I want to talk to the doctor myself."

She goes to call Dr. Duffner while I sit on the couch holding Hunter. He wasn't thriving like a typical four-month-old baby boy should, but we never in our darkest nightmares would have imagined this. A fatal genetic disease that will most likely end his life before he can celebrate his second birthday. Pain and sorrow engulf my heart and our home as my two-year-old daughter, Erin, stares into my tear-filled eyes, confused.

"What's wrong, Mommy? Why are you crying?" Erin asks, her beautiful gaze filled with wonder. Words won't come, so I reach out and grab her, trying to explain with my embrace. I'm clinging to my child filled with life as this gorgeous, innocent baby boy's life is stolen away with every heartbeat.

My mother's eyes blaze with relentless determination, fill with tears, and ache with anguish. "I can't believe it," she says as she walks back into the room. "I can't believe this. We're going to fight this thing, whatever it is. We'll figure this out, no matter what we have to do, Jill," she protests as she sits down next to Hunter. And as she runs her fingers through his wavy brown hair, she says again, "We're going to fight this. You're going to be just fine, Hunter. Everything is going to be okay," she says, tears cascading down her cheeks as she looks away.

⌒

She's going to do something about this—and she does. She leaves her six-figure job, the position she has worked so hard to achieve, to come alongside me and help take care of Hunter.

Of all the moments I cherish of my mother giving of herself, her time, talents, and treasure, none are more precious than watching her love my children, especially Hunter. Her love for Hunter surpassed any expectations I would have ever had for their relationship. In saying this, my point is that it wasn't just a love that a grandmother feels for her grandchild, as precious as that bond is. This was a love set apart, a love that everyone could see and feel when they were around my mother and Hunter. When they were together the warmth of that love would emanate from them, it was palpable and truly unforgettable. I learned how to be a better mom by watching my mother care for and be a grandmother to my three children. During the most devastating time of our family's journey, she stood strong and confident for all of us, even though I knew she wanted to crumble. The absolute necessity to feel her strength overshadowed any doubts that she may have been fearful or faltering.

One heroic memory of my mother I absolutely treasure and will never forget unfolded one night when Hunter was just three years old. He had taken a sudden turn for the worse and was desperately sick, struggling frantically to survive. His condition had deteriorated severely and his breathing was so shallow that we thought for sure he was going to die. We had done everything we knew to do for him at the time and with it so touch and go, we had to stand vigil through the night. In order to monitor his breathing as closely as we needed to, my mother and I took turns holding Hunter and comforting him. It was a long, dark night, but we did it together and Hunter ended up going into the hospital by ambulance early the next morning. I'll never forget that night with my mom. We cried, prayed, and even sang to Hunter all night long.

We did all of this together. There was no taking turns so one of us could rest; we combined our efforts to comfort Hunter together so he would be able to feel twice the mothers' love. That night—in that foxhole, so to speak—we were all giving and getting something we desperately needed from each other as we fought for Hunter's life.

My mom is an amazing woman. The love and friendship we share is a result of walking through heartbreak and suffering and enduring the unthinkable together. Had we not surrendered our lives to a purpose beyond ourselves, we might not be as close as we are today. Graciously, God intervened in both of our hearts and cradled our relationship firmly in His unfailing love. We became Christians around the same time. She was searching and longing to know God in a real way before Hunter got sick, and when he did, she stormed heaven for answers. I'm so thankful we were on the same page in our quest for truth and faith because had we not been, I'm sure our relationship would've suffered for a lot of reasons.

She's my best friend. She's the one who knows me better than anyone else and loves me anyway. My mother is the one who comes when I call, no matter what. She stands in the gap, no matter how deep, wide, or treacherous. Her prayers are fervent and she's always praying. Always. I don't ever have to ask her to pray because I know she's holding on to God, and she won't let go until He answers. And she's not only praying—she's rallying the troops to pray too, because she gets it. She gives.

All.

She.

Has.

And all she is.

I am continually in awe of her, and so grateful I have an anchor like her to keep me close to shore during the fury of the storms life rains down upon us. I'd give anything to have a person like this in my life, even if she wasn't my mother—but I thank God she is! She's my mom, my cheerleader, and the one I talk to every day about everything and anything. She didn't have to leave her job when Hunter got sick, but she did. She didn't have to take care of Hunter as often as she did so that I could get some rest, but she did—gladly. I want to be more like her, and pour out my life for the sake of others the way she does. I want to have a

generous heart that beats to encourage people and give in abundance—
a heart like my mom's.

The longer I walk with the Lord, the better I know Him. And the
better I know Him, the more I see how her heart reflects the character
and life of Jesus. I want to spend my life for the sake of making someone
else's day a little better, because that's what she does every day. When
I'm in line at the McDonald's drive-thru I want to buy lunch for the
strangers behind me or bless the worker with a huge smile because that's
what my mom does. All the time. Like her, I want to spread joy, and
regardless of how hectic life gets, make time to see things most people
miss because they're too busy. I want to listen, really listen, not just with
my ears, but with my heart. To stop and smell the roses—even if I have
to hold them by the thorns to do it.

Like she does.

⌒

"Mom, can I tell you something?" Erin says with a smile.

"Of course. What do you want to tell me, honey?" I respond.

"I hope this doesn't make you feel bad or anything, but I
love Grammie as much as I love you."

With a smile on my face and tears in my eyes I respond,
"Now you know how I feel, Erin. She's my mom and you loving
her just as much as me is why I love her like I do. You loving
Grammie as much as you do blesses me."

⌒

Erin loves my mother. They have such a close bond that I wouldn't
doubt it if Erin told my mother her deepest secrets, secrets she hasn't
even shared with me. Some mothers might be jealous or feel threatened,
indulging a sense of competition—a twisted drive to contend for the

hearts of their children. Not this mother. I was (and am) grateful beyond measure for the example, inspiration, and help my mother has been to my family and me.

How could I not treasure the same for my little lambs? Grammie is trustworthy and faithful, but she's not perfect, no one is (what a relief!). Her weaknesses and shortcomings are just another opportunity for her to display a trust in the Lord that makes you want to run to Him for everything. I can still feel the teenage tears and fears, the jealousy and the bad choices. I remember the days I wish I could forget. The pain of Hunter's diagnosis has never left, nor has the anguish of saying good-bye—I miss him every second of every minute of every hour of every day of every month of…you get the idea. I still ache in the frustration and heartbreak of a failed marriage, while my spirits soar in the joy of its gracious resurrection by the mercy of God.

And I remember that she was there for me in the midst of it all, routinely giving all she had—and then, somehow, finding even more to give.

And as believers, the inspiration of our hearts to give and give and give yet again is the Giver Himself, who reigns from the throne of our hearts that we have joyfully relinquished to Him, because He has given all for us.

⁓

The mood in our car erupted with anticipation as we turned into the parking lot and saw it absolutely packed. Suddenly I felt electric, as bright and brisk as the crystal-blue mid-morning sky. It was the "Hunter's Hope Every Step Walk for Universal Newborn Screening" (please check out the appendix for more information) and it looked like we were going to have a packed house—I was ecstatic. We eagerly tumbled out of the car.

"This is so great," I heard myself think out loud, almost gushing like a child with a shiny new toy. "A turnout like this is so awesome! More people will know and understand and help us fight this good fight for all the children." What I thought but couldn't bring myself to say aloud was, Help them never have to suffer like my Hunterboy.

I leaned into the breeze as it danced through the leaves—it felt as good as I knew this day was going to be. We excitedly made our way over to the designated area, where hundreds of people had gathered for the "Every Step Walk." Grinning from ear to ear, I glanced into the distance only to feel my smile melt away like wax from a flaming candle. There, on the other side of the park, was a crowd that dwarfed ours—wall-to-wall people who had gathered for another event that was sched- uled at the same time as our walk.

I strained my eyes to make out the signs, only to discover that the other affair was an event for dogs. The parking lot was full, but most of the crowd was over at the dog event in- stead of the walk where we were helping to raise money to save children's lives. To say that I was disappointed would be an epic understatement. As Jim, the girls, and I walked over to greet some of the Hunter's Hope staff, my mom and dad walked up to meet us.

"Okay, so when we pulled in I thought all the cars were for our event," I complained to my mother as she hugged me.

"I know, me too. But there's some big dog event happening. Did you bring Bella? You could go check it out when the walk is over." An eternal optimist, she's always positive; finding the upside in every situation. "Maybe all the dog owners will see our walkers and wonder what's up. Who knows? But certainly they're all here and so are we, so there must be a good rea- son for it." My mom knows me better than I know myself, and could tell how disappointed I was, so she continued to try to lift my spirits.

My introspective bubble abruptly burst. "Hi, Jill, can we get our picture taken with you?" a woman asked as she reached out to shake my hand.

"Of course. And who is this?" I joyfully replied, referring to the adorable baby girl nestled peacefully in the woman's arms. "This is MacKenzie and my husband, Brice, and I'm Nicole." As we moved in close for a photo, the event's emcee announced that it was time for all walkers to make their way over to the finish line for the start of the event. We snapped a quick picture as droves of people scattered around us and scurried over to get ready for the walk. Saying our good-byes, I turned to go but before I could, Nicole handed her baby girl to Brice, pivoted, and grabbed my arm. She held me with a desperation that stopped me in my tracks. Her eyes, full of tears, riveted me as she poured out her heart.

"I don't even know where to start. And I know the walk is about to begin and you need to get over there, but you need to know something. MacKenzie wouldn't be here if it were not for Hunter and what you and Jim are doing through newborn screening. She wouldn't be here." Tears streamed down her cheeks as she tried in vain to pull herself together. The announcer interrupted the moment with a final call for walkers, but God bless him, he was wasting his time. I wasn't going anywhere.

"Thank you for continuing to fight for children you don't even know, even though Hunter is gone. My daughter is alive because you chose to continue giving despite your loss. I don't know how you do it, Jill. I don't know how you and Jim continue to fight." Her trembling voice trailed off as she let go of my arm and I fell into hers, reaching out to hug her. We embraced and as she pulled away I thanked her through tears that fell in torrents of hope from my eyes. However many people may have gone to the dog-related event on the other side of the park, Nicole and I were a majority of hope. A hope that captivated the moment when disappointment and sorrow tried to rule the day . . .

Our foundation had pretty humble beginnings and was birthed in our living room with pizza, coffee, and tears attending the unassuming event. We had no idea where it would all go, but we wanted to do something to help fight this horrid disease so few people had ever heard of. Leveraging Jim's celebrity to make a difference seemed like a promising beginning. But it wasn't enough. We had to share our heartbreak and make our private struggles public as well, and that was tough—I didn't want to share my fears and tears with the world, but I was willing. However, there was one more sacrifice that came with the territory, and it was the hardest thing I'd ever given up—Hunter.

My tears, my private life, Jim's reputation—that was one thing, I could live with that. But not Hunter, I did not want to give Hunter to the world. I didn't want to allow personal photos—of his adorable face, of him snuggled in the arms of our family—those private treasures to be passed around among people who would never realize all they meant. I would dissolve into tears and fall apart at the end of events when I'd see his angelic face on discarded flyers, crumpled with dirty footprints, scattered like trash on the ground. It would just break me.

It took a long time for me to get used to giving Hunter to the public, to let them know him so we could fight for the lives of children we would never know. Yet, as agonizing as it was for so long, the more I learned to give of Hunter, the more God inspired me to give even more of him and myself.

In retrospect, I guess it was so hard because it was never about saving Hunter—it was always about saving other children and helping other families. And as our little foundation gathered momentum we were blessed with hundreds of letters penned by very grateful people thanking us for our sacrificial efforts. It meant a great deal to me but could not soothe the ache in my broken heart because our efforts, as aggressive and effective as they were, could not and would not save Hunter.

The thing is, I understood that we needed to live beyond ourselves, to tear open our comfort zones, and give of our time, treasure, and even our son—literally. But the longing of my heart was for my son to live; something I knew was not to be. Then I met Nicole and MacKenzie at the walk, a loving mother cradling her precious daughter in her arms because the baby's disease was caught in time through our efforts. New York's state-based public health system screens newborns to prevent the devastating consequences of a number of medical conditions not clinically recognizable at birth. All states do this to some measure, but the required diseases that are screened vary from state to state. MacKenzie's disease was discovered because the Hunter's Hope Newborn Screening effort led to New York State adding it to its screening program.

It was a watershed moment in my soul and I've never been the same. I knew how Nicole felt because my greatest loss was her greatest gain—her daughter was alive because my son suffered and died. And had we not given Hunter to this cause, this could not have been possible. But because we gave our one and only son, countless children will hopefully live to enjoy their lives, reach their potential, and fulfill their destinies.

We laid our Hunter on the altar and gave him back to God, albeit reluctantly. Yet in doing so, God moved us to give Hunter for a purpose bigger than ourselves, a purpose beyond anything we could have ever asked or imagined. A purpose that ultimately brought us to a hope greater than even a cure or treatment, a hope stretching beyond this fleeting life deep into the next. I don't mean to sound lofty or over the top, or fabricate meaning where there is none and the analogies break down. But simply put, it was through the giving of our only son, Hunter, that God brought us to His One and Only Son, Jesus, given to save the world. And in our finding Jesus, He began to teach us what true sacrificial giving is all about!

⌒

Giving. Maybe it really all boils down to love...

When we love much, we give much, and give with right motives, not out of guilt or compulsion, but inspired by sheer, unadulterated love. I can't help but recall a story in the Bible that has always been especially meaningful to me. It's about a woman who gave all she had. You might be familiar with her story, but it's worth repeating because her story can be your story—our story.

> Jesus was hanging out at the temple with His disciples (oh my goodness, don't you wish you were there watching Him in action?). Women were only allowed in the temple courts, so that was probably where Jesus was that day—that moment. There were a number of collection boxes in the temple for people to place their freewill offerings. On this particular day Jesus was watching.
>
> Jesus sat down opposite the place where the offerings were put and watched the crowd putting their money into the temple treasury. Many rich people threw in large amounts. But a poor widow came and put in two very small copper coins, worth only a fraction of a penny.
>
> Calling his disciples to him, Jesus said, "I tell you the truth, this poor widow has put more into the treasury than all the others. They all gave out of their wealth; but she, out of her poverty, put in everything—all she had to live on." (Mark 12:41–44)

Clearly, the value of our gift isn't determined by the amount we give as much as the heart from which we give it—and God knows our hearts. He knows the motivation behind every single act of generosity and He's not nearly as concerned with *how much* we give as He is about *how and why we give*. When we give grudgingly, or to create a spiritual perception that wins the praise of men, then our gift loses its value. It ends up being worthless in spite of its dollar amount or material value.

But when God is involved and we give out of our gratitude to Him for all He has given, it changes everything, and He is exalted rather than man. It's not about the gift, it's about the giver. The thing is (and you can take this to the bank—pun intended, sorry), Jesus isn't just referring to our bankbook balance. He didn't walk among us, die upon a cross, and rise again three days later for money, to pad our bank accounts so that we could fill up the collection plate. There is no "Lord, Inc." and in fact, He had to borrow a coin to illustrate a point He was making while He was teaching because His pockets were empty (see Mark 12:14–17).

No, He gave His life as an example for us so that we might give ours. That means exactly what it means. He gave us an example to follow, giving His life every day all the way to the cross, so we'd understand why and how to give ours. He first loved us, deeply and recklessly, so we would love with the same wild abandon. He forgave so we would forgive as liberally and passionately. He prayed feverishly so we'd understand its value and pray with all we have. He risked it all to show us how much we meant, so we could be confident and bold in our love, and risk showing others.

It's the motivation filling the heart; the why behind the giving, *that's* what matters most, and God knows if we're sincere or manipulative. He is the ultimate Giver, every good and perfect gift comes from Him (see James 1:17). Just as love, forgiveness, and suffering originate in Him, so too does the very nature of giving. For God so loved the world that He gave—love comes *before* giving, and purifies our motives (see John 3:16).

And giving that is driven by love is critical for a lot of reasons, a big one being that giving comes with a cost and a risk. You never know for sure before you give whether or not the receiver will acknowledge or appreciate the gift. So in any situation we have to weigh the risk and decide if we're willing and able to take it.

Consider Jesus. He gave the ultimate gift, His very life, knowing in advance that many would never accept it. He knew that some would mock His sacrifice; others would deny it and say He never even gave His life in the first place. Knowing all this, He still gave everything He had—He took the risk.

Maybe He took it all down to the bone because He knew exactly who would repent, believe, and receive. And because of the joy in knowing that they would gratefully unwrap His priceless gift, He endured and went to the cross despite those who would stiff-arm the love He gave so freely.

When we *know* that we're secure and sure of *what we hope for* . . . when we are *certain* of *what we do not see* . . . when we *resolutely believe* that God *is*—and that He *will* reward those who seek *Him* (not the things He can give us) . . . *then* we can take that step of *faith and risk* rejection and hurt. When we know Christ and understand all *He gave*, then we can see Him moving in *our giving*.

And *we* can exhale and give—unreservedly, wholeheartedly, no matter what the cost—and we can *live* by faith. For once you've given your life, there's nothing you *won't* give, there's nothing else *to* give—you've given it all.

You've already given *yourself* to Him . . .

Because He's worth the risk.

What to Remember and Never Forget . . .

- God is the ultimate Giver—the Giver of all good things. Everything you have, even your very breath, is a gift from Him.
- Our giving should first and foremost stem from our love for God.

- Christ is the perfect life example of what it looks like to give.
- Why you give is more important than what you give.

Prayer...

> *O Lord, You gave it all—You gave Yourself to save me, to get me out of the mess my life was and to get the mess out of me! I pray You'd give me the selfless, giving heart that You have. Cleanse me of covetousness, self-centeredness, and self-will. Help me see the surpassing value in being the difference, in investing in eternity, and living in the reality that the most valuable things aren't things at all. Make of me a giver, make me like You.*

Truths about Giving to Etch Upon Your Heart:

> Out of the most severe trial, their overflowing joy and their extreme poverty welled up in rich generosity. For I testify that they gave as much as they were able, and even beyond their ability. (2 Corinthians 8:2–3)

> For you know the grace of our Lord Jesus Christ, that though he was rich, yet for your sakes he became poor, so that you through his poverty might become rich. (2 Corinthians 8:9)

> For if the willingness is there, the gift is acceptable according to what one has, not according to what he does not have. (2 Corinthians 8:12)

> Remember this: Whoever sows sparingly will also reap sparingly, and whoever sows generously will also reap

generously. Each man should give what he has decided in his heart to give, not reluctantly or under compulsion, for God loves a cheerful giver. (2 Corinthians 9:6–7)

You will be made rich in every way so that you can be generous on every occasion, and through us your generosity will result in thanksgiving to God. (2 Corinthians 9:11)

chapter six

prayer

True prayer does not depend either on the individual or the whole body of the faithful, but solely upon the knowledge that our Heavenly Father knows our needs. That makes God the sole object of our prayers, and frees us from a false confidence in our own prayerful efforts.
                                    Dietrich Bonhoeffer

I asked Jim if I could get away and get quiet with God—so I could listen, hear, and write. I don't know why, but writing this book has me broken, needy. There have been more distractions and interruptions during this season than I can count.

Hunter's Haven Lodge is a snowy fortress hidden in wilderness. It's the perfect place to write—or at least I hope it will be. I've never written anywhere other than in my office at home. This is something altogether new. I ponder and think to myself, maybe this is why there were so many distractions. God wanted to bring me here.

There's a fire blazing in the hearth and in my heart—I need to hear from God today. I grab my journal and Bible and do what I do every day. But this is not going to be just another quiet time. It can't be. I'm here to pray and write, and like Jacob, I won't let go until the blessings flow. I'm ready to wrestle, or at least I think I am.

I pray and ask God to show me what's on His heart, what He wants me to write, what He longs to communicate to the reader. I open His Word and pray more using His very words. Except for the crackling of wood in the fireplace, it's quiet, and I'm thankful. I trust that He will tell me what to write next.

Before I get on the computer, I grab the book I've been reading and start in where I left off the night before.

"Empty Stomach . . . There is more than one way to draw a prayer circle. In fact, sometimes it involves more than prayer. I believe fasting is a form of circling. In fact, an empty stomach may be the most powerful prayer posture in Scripture."[1]

I stop reading and think, "Wait a minute, I'm fasting right now." My stomach reminds me of this with a loud growl that makes my Chihuahua Bella jump off my lap.

I continue reading.

"Even Jesus said that some miracles are not possible via prayer. Some miracles are only accessible via prayer and fasting. It takes the combination of prayer and fasting to unlock some double dead bolts."[2]

I stop reading and grab my journal. I might not need a miracle, but it just might take one to finish this manuscript on time.

I get back to reading.

"When I need a breakthrough, I circle it with a fast. It doesn't just break down the challenges I'm facing; it also breaks down the calluses in my heart. Maybe there is something you've been praying for that you need to fast for."[3]

"Yes, exactly. I need a breakthrough, like right now, for this book. Search me, Lord. Break down the calluses," I whisper a prayer.

I keep reading and reading.

"The physical discipline gives you the spiritual discipline to pray through. An empty stomach leads to a full spirit. The tandem of prayer and fasting will give you the power and willpower to pray through until you experience a breakthrough."[4]

And then it happens. A breakthrough happens in the midst of the reading and God tells me what to write about next. Prayer. It's like the writer's block dam broke and I can hardly contain the flood of words that begin to pour out. I write and write . . . and write some more. I remember moments vividly. I keep writing. But then I stop. Something in my spirit moves me to go back to reading the book. And so I do.

"Ten Steps to Goal Setting: Goals are as unique as we are. They should reflect our unique personalities and passions."[5]

A thought interrupts my reading, You know what you're going to write about now. You don't need to keep reading. You don't need to learn about goal setting right now. I ignore the thought and continue reading.

> "Start with prayer. Prayer is the best way to jump-start the process of goal setting. I highly recommend a personal retreat of fasting. I came up with my original life goal list during a two-day retreat at Rocky Gap Lodge."[6]

I stop reading and drop to my knees. Tears roll down my cheeks and joy fills my heart as praise and gratitude pour from my lips.

"Oh my goodness, thank you, God. I'm on a two-day retreat. I'm fasting and praying. I'm at a lodge. Thank you for meeting me here, right now. Thank you for being so faithful and good." I continued to pray and thank Him.

⌒

Please don't tell me you think this was just a coincidence—there's no such thing. This was a God-ordained God incident. I had no idea what was going to happen at the lodge during my two-day retreat. All I knew was this: there was writing that needed to be done (for the book you're holding right now) and I was desperate for God to lead the way, to reveal His heart and pour life through me onto paper. Little did I know that during this time of intimate prayer and fasting I would end up writing this chapter on prayer and fasting. All of what you will read in this chapter was birthed during my time at the lodge. For whatever reason, maybe because He's incredibly good and faithful, or maybe because He wanted to reveal Himself to me (and now you) in a very intimate way, whatever the reason, I know this—you're holding the result.

This was my first real fast. Yes, I had fasted in the past but never to the extent that I did during the two-day lodge retreat. There was truth revealed at the lodge that I don't want you to miss.

I didn't really understand fasting before this. I had read what Jesus said about it in the New Testament but never really got it, at least not to the extent that I do now. You can find some insight about fasting in the book of Matthew. "When you fast, do not look somber as the hypocrites do" (Matt. 6:16, see also 17–18). You don't have to read very far to get the point. Jesus didn't say *"if* you fast" or "if you *feel* like fasting." He said *"when* you fast." Jesus talks about fasting in other places in the New Testament as well. He even fasted for forty days Himself. Clearly, every single move Jesus made, everything He did and continues to do, has purpose and meaning. Jesus never does something just for the sake of doing it and neither should we. His followers should fast, and for many good reasons, the most important being to know Him more intimately.

As I've already said at least a dozen times, God isn't finished with me yet. He's not finished with you either—there are more moments to be lived. He is endless and eternal. We are limited. And because we have a very narrow capacity to know and understand eternal truths, God reveals what we need to know when we need to know it; as we're ready to receive it. Maybe my heart wasn't ready to receive, understand, and put into practice what prayer in conjunction with fasting is all about when Hunter was with us. If I knew and understood, you'd better believe I would've fasted. I would have done anything for that boy. Maybe God knew my body, mind, and soul would not be able to handle abstaining during that season of my life.

Maybe you're reading this and feel the Spirit of God nudging you to do your own fast. Maybe not. I don't know. But what I do know is this— He will finish the good work He started in your life as well as the good work He began in mine. And part of that good work includes fasting, like today, right now, while I pray and write the rest of this book. But we would do well to never forget God's heart in these spiritual mandates.

Among the most electrifying and powerful rewards of the Spirit's toil in our lives is His effort to form the image of God Himself in our hearts. That in the mystery of redemption, clay might again cover the purity, radiance, and glory of the Lord. In the end, all the prayer, fasting, good works, sacrifice, and love bring us to this precious, inescapable net effect: "Christ in you, the hope of glory" (Col. 1:27).

Before we go any further, there's something you need to know. Prayer is not about you! Shocking, I know, but true. If prayer were about anything other than God it would be empty and meaningless. We find everything we need in Him. Our deepest longings of heart and soul are satisfied in Christ alone. So let me say it one more time (and please don't throw this book across the room):

Prayer is not about you, it's about God!

For that very reason it would be impossible for me to sum up the treasure of all that prayer is and all I've learned in one chapter. Just as I was unable to communicate the depth of what love, suffering, and everything else we've shared here so far is. It's bigger than a chapter. It's bigger than a bazillion books, for that matter—it's beyond us. But what I do hope to do, like I've done in the previous chapters, is share moments of what learning about prayer looked like through my journey of faith thus far. (I'm going to interject another disclaimer here—I'm not a theology major. I don't have this all figured out. Go ask a pastor. No, seriously, seek the heart and wisdom of God through His Word. If You seek Him, you'll find Him. I promise. Another disclaimer—don't take my word for it, take Him at His Word and trust HIM.) Oddly, and I think you'll find this to be true in your life too, sometimes we learn who God is through the revelation of who He's not. He allows us to experience what self-centered praying is so that we come to want more of Him and less of ourselves.

~

"Make sure you say your prayers before you go to bed," Mother yelled from the kitchen.

"What for?" I mumbled like a storm cloud softly thundering, as I walked into the bathroom to brush my teeth. Before I climbed into blankets, I knelt down beside my bed and prayed:

"In the name of the Father, Son, and the Holy Spirit. Dear God, I pray for my mom, dad, brother, and my dog. Please protect them and don't let anything bad happen to them ever. Please help me to be a good, sweet, kind little girl and help me to make the right decisions always. 'Our Father, who art in heaven, hallowed be thy name. Thy kingdom come, thy will be done, on earth as it is in heaven. Give us this day our daily bread and lead us not into temptation, but deliver us from evil. For thine is the kingdom and the power and the glory, now and forever.'"

~

For most of my life, up until roughly a decade ago, my prayer life has always revolved around me and my desires. It was about what I wanted from God even more so than what I needed from Him. Prayer was what my parents did. It was what I was taught to do in parochial school as well as what we did in church on Sunday mornings. It saddens me to say this but it's true, before I knew what I know now—if I didn't have a reason to pray, I didn't. In other words, if it wasn't about me or something that concerned me, there was no need to pray about it. Isn't this sad? Or is it? Maybe the selfish, all-about-me praying would be the vehicle God would use to draw me into a real, authentic relationship. Real prayer. Only in time, at just the right moment, would the greater need of an empty, desperate heart be revealed. And it would be exposed through my greatest heartbreak and deepest joy—the life and suffering of my one and only son, Hunter.

In view of this distasteful morsel of my personal history, please tell me I'm not the only one who lived a self-consumed, narcissistic life before Jesus intervened to save the day. Before I felt led or had a legitimate reason to actually pray hard, my prayer life consisted of four prayers: the Hail Mary, the Our Father, the Glory Be, and the sort of prayer I just shared. Please hear my heart right now, I'm very thankful for my Roman Catholic upbringing. Jesus teaches us in the Gospels how to pray what we call "the Our Father." But praying the Our Father without knowing the Father isn't really praying at all, is it? I mean, even a parrot could be taught to recite it! God is sovereign. And in His indescribable, perfect wisdom, mercy, and grace, His plan for me (and maybe for you too) was to first learn the way of religion before being captivated by relationship.

I hope you're not shaking your head right now or flipping to the back of the book to look for a way to connect with me so you can scold me. Again, please step out of what you know and understand in this moment and try to receive this. It was part of His plan. I don't know why, but I do know, beyond a shadow of doubt, that God has ordained every single moment in our lives before one of them came to be. Before you took life's first breath, the script for your entire life was written. Every day ordained for you was already written in His book before the sun rose on even one of them (see Ps. 139:16).

None of it is in vain. God knew what He was doing. He never says "oops!" And at the end of the day—no, at the beginning, middle, end, and every single second in between—it's all about Him. Maybe it's our need, our times of desperation, those moments of weakness and fear. Maybe it's those very moments, like the one you'll read next, when God begins to woo us to Himself. Regardless of the maybes, it's through one circumstance at a time that He leads us into one prayer at a time, one minute at a time, where He draws us into all that He is. And all that He truly is can only be found at the end of who we are. All that we are apart from Him can only be exposed through a "work all things together for good" God. A "mighty to save" God who made a way for us to come to Him and to know Him more through His One and Only Son. But we don't always get this, do we? For some of us it takes a lifetime; and yet He created time and knows exactly how long it will take.

⌒

Hard heels pound against wood as she walks toward the door. "What in the world am I doing here?" I murmur under my breath as the door swings open in front of me.

"Come in," she says and turns to walk down the hallway. The stench of mothballs fills the air and already I can't wait to get out of there. She leads me into a small room where gloom, a desk, and two chairs await me. "Father John will be right with you. You can have a seat right here," she explains, pointing in the direction of the two old leather chairs resting side by side in front of the desk. I can't help but think she already knows what I did, but how could she? Her icy presence sends chills down my spine. My hands start to sweat, and my body fidgets uncontrollably.

The leather squeaks as I try to get comfortable in the brittle chair. I'm a nervous wreck. How will comfort be found when my tumultuous heart is in a whirlwind searching for help, hope, anything to lift this burden of guilt that's crushing me? The rehearsal of the conversation I'm about to have with the stranger of the cloth plays over and over again in my mind. "I made a really bad decision. And I don't know what to do about it." As the tape rolls on in my head, Father John enters the office.

Without a handshake or formal greeting he sits down behind the desk. It seems like minutes of deadening silence crawl by while I wait to unload my heart.

"So tell me why you're here. What happened?" he asks in a wooden, emotionless voice. Before I can say a word, the phone rings and he answers it. "Sure, tell him I'll call him back soon. This shouldn't take too long." Shouldn't take too long! Are you kidding me? My heart is ready to explode. I came here to pour out the anguish of my soul, to unload the burden of guilt and shame I've been dragging around. And he says it's not going to take too long! I should've seized the moment and bolted out of there as fast as I could. But I didn't. I stayed in the cold leather chair while Father John stared a hole right through me.

The depth of my shame gushed out faster than my mind could tell my mouth to communicate, and within seconds I was in a puddle of tears. Father John said nothing. He waited and watched while I tried to pull myself together. "My boyfriend . . . we were smoking pot and then everything got out of control. I couldn't think straight. I didn't tell him to stop. I didn't stop him. I knew what he was doing was wrong. I should've told him not to take what he did, but I couldn't. And now I'm in huge trouble. My parents are going to kill me and . . ."

"And what do you want me to do about it? What makes you think I can help you?" he interrupted callously. His fierce tone turned my stomach sour and I felt like I might throw up.

"Well, I thought I should come to you to confess what I've done. I was hoping God might help me."

"I don't know what God's going to do with you. You need

to pray and you can start with the Rosary. Do it over and over again. That's what you need to do. And then maybe you will be forgiven."

~

It took a long time for me to shake this one. This moment and the details of my attempted act of contrition are still deeply etched upon my heart. As you can imagine, my understanding of religion and everything God took a nosedive after the Father John meeting. Over and over again for years the entire scenario played out in my mind. I contemplated what I could've said differently and what I wished I had kept to myself.

It was all foolishness to me at the time, because I was perishing—Jesus wasn't even on my radar screen. Or was He? Was the running to the priest from Him? Can the fingerprints of God be found in my seeking after forgiveness in the only way I knew how at that time? Would this be the breakthrough moment when I would start to learn what prayer and the Author of it looks like? Not quite.

Sometimes we need to experience who God is not in order to know who He truly is.

The truth is, Father John was right, he couldn't help me. Nothing that he told me to do or not do in that moment made any difference—or did it? Believe it or not I'm thankful for Father John. I'm serious. I'm thankful that he didn't have all the answers for me, because *religion is never the answer*. Furthermore, God doesn't forgive us any more or less because we ask Him to. And He doesn't forgive us any more or any less because we screw up royally and pray a few hundred beads on a rosary. He forgives because He's God. Nothing we can do or not do will make Him love us any more or less. He loves us because He *is* LOVE. No amount of anything that we do or say will change this. Nothing in all creation can separate us from the love of God that is in Christ Jesus our Lord. He loves us infinitely, forever, and always, no matter what. He doesn't weigh our good deeds against our bad choices. Somebody needs to shout "amen" right now.

Obviously, I didn't have a better grasp or understanding of God or prayer after I left Father John's office that day. But what I did carry with me, deep within my heart of hearts, was a longing for something more. More than what I understood about the things of God in that moment. More than just some words prayed that meant absolutely nothing to me. I longed for more of what I didn't know in that moment. God knew this, so He sent the more we all search for. He sent His Son. And in time, at just the right moment, He sent mine.

The church was full so it took the usher a few minutes to find a place for us to sit. He found room in the far back right, four rows in from the last row in the sanctuary. This was where we usually sat when we were able to make it to Sunday service. We had a nurse that day to care for Hunter so we were able to go. My parents decided to travel in as well. They loved going to our church whenever they could. As we moved in and filled our row, the words from one of our favorite worship songs filled the room and my heart. "I could sing of your love forever . . . I could sing of your love forever . . ." It was one of our all-time favorites for two reasons: first, Hunter's best friend, Robert, always sang this song whenever he would come over for a playdate, and second, this was the only song Hunter's Christian band, The Hopesters, ever learned to play together.

It was never easy for me to be away from Hunter. I always felt like I was in a rush to get home to be near him; to make sure he was okay. This moment in church was no different. I made every effort to soak in the good news the pastor was preaching, but my heart and mind were filled with thoughts of my sick son waiting for me at home. At the end of the service Pastor Greg made a call for family prayer. Family prayer is a time set aside at the end of the service to pray for specific needs in the congregation. Pastor Greg asked, "If you have a pressing need right now, any burden weighing heavily upon your heart that you need prayer for, please lift up your hand so we can see you. And if everyone around these people would move in to lay hands on them that would be great."

You would've thought he said, "Jill Kelly, come up here to the altar, please." I was a nervous wreck. Of course I needed prayer; my only son was being robbed of life every single day. I started sweating as the people in the pew in front of us turned in our direction. As they moved toward us I thought to myself, Wow, I don't even have to raise my hand, they already know we need prayer. But then I turned and looked to my right where my mother was standing. Her hand was raised! Within seconds we were surrounded. I reached over and placed my hand on my mother's shoulder as Pastor Greg began to pray. Tears poured down my cheeks. I tried to concentrate on what the pastor was saying but I was distracted. Shocked, I stared in stunned disbelief, unable to fathom that my mother had raised her hand for prayer—especially since my father was standing right next to her.

After the prayer ended and everyone went back to their seats, I leaned over and whispered in my mother's ear, "I'm so proud of you." She pulled back, grabbed my hand, looked into my eyes, and said these words, driven with a conviction that I would never forget: "I will raise my hands for Hunter anytime, anywhere."

Anytime.

Anywhere.

My prayer life changed that day.

She raised her hand. I didn't.

I was not only proud of her; I was also taken aback. This was not how we were taught. This was not how we did church or prayer—we never raised our hands for prayer. In fact, we never raised our hands in church for anything but to shake hands with the people sitting near us during the extending of peace. In order to understand what I'm talking about, you would have to come from a Roman Catholic background. If you did, then you know exactly what I'm referring to. We didn't do this kind of stuff in church.

But then Hunter got sick; everything changed. Everything—including prayer. After I began a relationship with God through Jesus, one of the first things I needed to learn and understand was prayer. What is it and how in the world do I do it? What's the formula? Do I close my eyes and kneel beside my bed? I was clueless. Saying "Hail Marys" and "Our Fathers" around the Rosary wasn't enough. Hunter was dying. Prayer had to be more than repetition; it had to be more than memorized words. It had to be more than everything I understood prayer to be because Hunter's life depended on it. My life depended on it.

My mother and I hadn't been Christians for very long at this point in time, so we were just getting used to the concept of people laying hands on us and praying. We were still learning and growing in our relationship with Christ (and we're *still* learning and growing). This was all new, and to be honest, we were sort of freaked out.

Sometimes it takes someone else's boldness to ignite a fire in our own hearts. My hand should've been waving in the air. Actually I should've been jumping up and down for prayer for Hunter. He needed prayer every single day for the entire eight and a half years that God allowed him to live on earth. We all needed prayer. It wasn't that I didn't think we needed it; we were desperate for intercession. It was just all so new to me and somewhat intimidating and foreign.

Label it pride or whatever you want to call it, the way I see it now, looking back on that moment etched upon my heart, God was teaching me how to pray. School of Prayer 101 was in session, and I needed to know just how important it was that I could come boldly to the throne of grace to find help in my time of need. My precious mother raising her hand during family prayer time was a tender nudging from the Lord to come boldly to His throne. My heart and mind needed to understand what I could only start to comprehend in that moment: when you need prayer and there's a call for you to be prayed for—go get it. Raise your hand. Run to the front of the altar. If you need it—go get it, as fast as you can. Don't hold back! Don't let anything stand in the way of prayer, and don't give up. Never. Ever!

We never stopped praying for Hunter. We prayed for his healing until the day the Lord healed him. No, God didn't heal Hunter like we had prayed and hoped He would. He never got up out of his wheelchair and walked. He never smiled or spoke a single word. (Just the thought of what his first word to Jesus was absolutely crushes me—I can't even imagine.) But God did heal Hunter. He ushered him into perfect healing the moment he breathed his last breath here on earth. God also healed our family in more ways than we can count; the first and most important being our salvation. The infinite ways of God are beyond our finite comprehension, and we must never forget that. For though He reasons with us, even created reason, His perspective is based upon an eternal value system that we spend a lifetime learning. So the way God reasons and makes decisions are often at odds with our temporal values, a way of thinking rooted in time, and what we predicate our decisions on.

I had a lot to learn that day in the sanctuary, and I still do—God isn't finished with me yet. He's not finished with you either. We all have so much more to learn, more treasures to discover. More lifting of our hands for prayer, more tears of brokenness turned into boldness before His throne to experience. I'd be lying if I said that I'm completely comfortable stepping out of my prayer comfort zone. I'm not. But I want to be and I continue to seek after His heart. I long for God to shatter every barrier in my prayer relationship with Him. I long for prayer to be less of me and more of Him in every way possible. My prayer life changed the day my mother raised her hand for Hunter and I'll never forget it. But this journey of life isn't over, and God continues to make Himself known to us in the moments, like the moment my firstborn prayed for her daddy.

"Come on in, sweet pea, the water's perfect. Hunter says, 'Hurry up, sissy, so we can play,'" I smiled and said to Erin. She climbed carefully into the bathtub as I gently moved Hunter out of the way.

"Let's pour some bubbles in and turn on the jets so we can hide behind all the bubbles!" She laughs. "And then Daddy will come in and try to find us. Come on, Mommy, it will be so funny."

"What do you think, Hunterboy? Should we do the bubbles and hide from Daddy?" I ask my son and look at him for a response.

He blinks once for "yes" and Erin erupts with joy.

"Thank you, HB. I knew you would say yes to the bubbles," Erin shouts as she moves in close to give her brother a kiss. "I love kissing your soft, chunky cheeks, brother." Erin loves on Hunter as I pour bubbles into the water. "Jets, Mommy, can I press the jets? Please!" she pleads with a big smile.

"Of course. Go ahead," I reply, smiling back.

Within minutes the bathtub is overflowing with bubbles. We

hear Daddy walking down the hall toward the bathroom, so we quickly hide behind our bubble mound.

"Where in the world did Mommy, Erin, and Hunter go?" he wonders, pretending not to see us. "Hmm, I see a lot of bubbles but no Mommy, Erin, and..."

"Here I am, Daddy!" Erin interrupts with excitement. Covered in bubbles, she looks like a snowman—or maybe a bubbleman.

"You guys look like you're having a lot of fun in there," Jim says as he kneels down next to the edge of the bathtub.

"Come on in, Daddy," Erin responds. She scoops up a handful of bubbles and puts it on the end of Jim's nose. "Look how silly you look, Daddy."

"Yes, I sure do look silly, don't I?" Jim responds, walking over to the mirror to look at the bubbles on the end of his nose. "Maybe next time I'll get in, Erin. I have to go help with dinner so I'll be back to check on you guys in a little bit. Okay?"

"Okay, Daddy." She grins as Jim walks out of the bathroom.

Erin puts her head down and turns away from us. Thinking that she's disappointed, I scoot Hunter and myself closer to her and put my hand on her back. "Honey, maybe you and Daddy can have a big bubble war sometime," I say with excitement, hoping to distract her.

"Shh, I'm praying," she responds.

"What are you praying about, Erin?" I ask with surprise.

She turns back around to face me. With a determined look on her face she says, "Mom, we don't know when Jesus is coming back. We don't know. We need to pray with Daddy tonight. We need to pray with him so that he can know Jesus. Mommy, we have to pray with Daddy as soon as we get out of the Jacuzzi. Okay?"

Her words pierce my heart. It's true; we don't know when Jesus is coming back, and she doesn't want her daddy to be left behind. I can't help but ponder her sense of urgency as we get out of the bath and ready for bed.

She continues to press the issue while I dry her brother off. "We need to pray with Daddy tonight, Mommy. We can't wait. We don't know when He's coming back," she insists.

"Why don't you ask Daddy to pray with you?" I say to her, hoping she'll let it go and save it for another time. But she doesn't let it go. She calls her dad and asks him to come pray with her.

"Daddy, come here, please," she shouts down the hallway. Before Jim can get through the door she's all over him, jumping up and down with excitement. "Mommy's getting Hunter ready for bed, so can you please pray with me?" she says as she leads him over to her bed.

We share a room, so I can hear everything she's saying to her father. "Daddy, do you want to ask Jesus into your heart? All you have to do is repeat after me. Okay, Daddy?" she asks Jim. I can hardly contain myself as I listen to Erin lead her dad in prayer. "Okay, Daddy, all you have to do is repeat after me. Just say what I say. Dear Jesus. You are the best and I love you. I need you to help me to live for You. Please forgive me and come into my heart. In Your Name I pray, amen."

"Okay, you need to go to sleep, silly girl. Daddy loves you." Jim gets up from Erin's bed and comes over to kiss Hunter and me good night. As soon as he leaves the room, Erin starts jumping up and down on her bed. "The angels are praising God in heaven right now. The angels are praising God in heaven," she says over and over with excitement as she jumps up and down.

I leave Hunter's side and run over to Erin. As I scoop her

up in my arms and hold her tight she grabs both of my cheeks with her little hands and looks into my eyes. "Mommy, did you know that angels start praising God in heaven when somebody asks God to forgive them and when Jesus comes into their heart?" She can hardly talk straight she's so excited.

"No, I didn't know that, Erin. That's amazing," I say excitedly and start jumping up and down on the bed with her.

⌒

Childlike faith.

Erin was seven years old when she prayed with her dad to invite Jesus into his heart. By faith, she was moved by the Spirit to pray and she did. There was no contemplating, rationalizing, or hoop jumping. Erin didn't think she had to prove herself to God in some way before she could come to Him. As if any sort of good works would've made her prayers more acceptable to God. Erin Marie understood at a very young age that she was part of a bigger family. She believed she was a princess of the King with an all-access pass behind the curtain and into the throne room through Jesus. Clothed in righteousness she could never earn or obtain in and of herself, her prayers were indicative of her faith. She prayed like she was part of the family because through Christ she was (and is).

She was compelled to pray earnestly and with urgency. It didn't matter to her how she prayed or what she prayed, and there was no formal presentation of contrived words. She prayed with childlike faith, conviction, and great confidence, as if she were sitting on her Heavenly Father's lap. I doubt she wondered whether or not God would answer her prayer or her daddy's prayer. She believed and felt the heartbeat of the Lord's love as her love for her earthly father moved her to do something about it. Sometimes I think we maximize our circumstances and minimize the greatness and sovereignty of God. It's as if whatever it is we're going through is too big for Him. Circumstances may *seem* so powerful because we can see and feel them, and they're so much bigger than we are. God, on the other hand, may *seem* so powerless because we cannot see Him and circumstances often seem to unfold in a way we deem inconsistent with our view and perception of love. But again, we see through a glass darkly, through time-colored glasses—the Lord looks at the eternal implications of our circumstances. The way what happens in time will shape our eternity. It's not a question of circumstances being greater than Him— He's God. It's about the way He shapes them to bring us deeper into His love, where we can draw near to Him through redemption and salvation by grace through faith in His Son, Jesus. With Him all things are possible for those who believe (see Mark 9:23).

We would not see the full manifestation of Erin's prayer until many years later, but I believe with all my heart that God received her childlike confession of faith and honored Jim's prayer with her that night. He blessed Erin's willingness and boldness. He motivated and inspired her tender heart to pray with urgency, because no one knows but the Father when Jesus will return. So why wait? Why not now? Don't wait to pray big, audacious prayers. Don't hesitate to pray and believe for the prodigal son or daughter. Don't let a diagnosis or deep disappointment allow fear to block faith. Stop letting your doubt trump His mercy and grace. He's God. Nothing is impossible for Him. Nothing! He owns the cattle on a thousand hills, He determines the number of stars and calls them out by name, tells the ocean waves they can only go so far (see Ps. 50:10 and 147:4). He watches over the sparrow and knows the moment the doe births her fawn—life exists because He is (see Matt. 6:26, Job 39:1). Nothing is too hard for Him (see Jer. 32:27).

For many years Erin would write "trust Jesus" anywhere and everywhere. I would find her little reminders in the most peculiar places. Oddly, but certainly not coincidentally, God would have me stumble upon a "trust Jesus" reminder exactly when I needed to trust Him more. I think that's what my daughter's prayer life exemplified most in her younger years—a childlike faith of trusting in Jesus. She seemed to understand the greater, deeper message that Jesus was trying to communicate to His disciples. "People were bringing little children to Jesus for him to place his hands on them, but the disciples rebuked them. When Jesus saw this, he was indignant. He said to them, 'Let the little children come to me, and do not hinder them, for the kingdom of God belongs to such as these. Truly I tell you, anyone who will not receive the kingdom of God like a little child will never enter it.' And he took the children in his arms, placed his hands on them and blessed them" (Mark 10:13–16).

I love this story. While there are probably countless theology scholars that can exegete these verses with multiple meanings, I find it pretty simple. And I have my daughter Erin and her prayer to remind me of the power of what this passage of Scripture spoken by the Word Himself is trying to convey. Come to Him, with everything and anything. Don't let anything or anyone (including yourself) hinder you from coming to Jesus in prayer. Don't try to use words you think He wants to hear. He already knows what you're going to say before you say it. It's not about the words—He's listening to the cry of your heart. He knows every hidden motive and agenda you have. It's all about Him, and He beckons you to come just as you are. With faith like a child reaching up to the Father—who's already reaching down—no strings attached. He made the ultimate sacrifice so you could come. One of my favorite authors, Oswald Chambers, said it best this way, "Let us never forget that our prayers are heard not because we are in earnest, not because we suffer, but because Jesus suffered."[7]

Another beautiful and extravagant truth I believe God taught me about prayer the night Erin prayed is this: she rejoiced! She literally jumped up and down after she prayed with her daddy. She started celebrating with the angels. In her heart and mind it was a done deal. Finished. Oh my goodness, I feel like I could jump up and down and out of my skin right now. This is huge. Erin by faith believed so deeply her heart leaped for joy and she immediately praised God for answering her prayer as well as her father's. I'm reminded right now of Jesus' last words on the cross, "It is finished" (John 19:30). And it is. Jesus accomplished everything that needed to be satisfied in order for us to know Him and have a relationship with the Father. Everything we need to pray and believe that His good and perfect will is going to be done on earth as it is in heaven. So pray earnestly with urgency and believe. And before you receive the answers, get on that bed and start jumping up and down until you can't jump anymore. The angels are already praising God (see Luke 15:7). Get jumping and join them! Because "we don't know when He's coming back."

One more thing before we move on. Maybe right now you're thinking about what you've wrestled with and prayed about in the past—if prayer is all about God, why does He want us to pray without ceasing, come boldly to His throne in our time of need, devote ourselves to prayer and fasting? Does this mean that God doesn't care about all that's going on in my life right now? If it's all about Him and not about me, then why should I even bother to take my fears and tears to Him?

Well, the answer is actually in the question. Our greatest need and gift *is* God—to know Him. The circumstances in our lives are the vehicles that drive us deeper into who He is. He knows we need Him so He tells us to seek Him in prayer where we will find Him. Knowing that prayer is all about God should move us to pray even more, not less.

He wants to show up, to reveal more of who He is to you in the midst of your moments. That's why we pray. That's why we fast—to see God and know Him as He really is. And when we see Him, we can't help but love Him and long to know Him more. God loves to bless us through answering our prayers. But the greatest blessing He gives, the one we need more than any other, is more of Him. And so we pray more to see more of Him in the midst of the moments we will always remember.

And those we'll never forget...

What to Remember and Never Forget...

- Prayer is not about you. It's about God—and you getting to know Him more. It's about the relationship He desires to have with you.
- Although we don't know exactly how or when God will answer, He will always answer our prayers. Always!
- Jesus made a way for you to come boldly to the Father in prayer. He wants you to know Him. When you know Him more you will pray with boldness. Because nothing is impossible for God.
- Pray without ceasing. Don't give up. Pray earnestly with urgency.
- God loves to bless us through answering our prayers. But the greatest blessing He gives, the one we need more than any other, is more of Him.

Prayer...

My friend, the prayer in this chapter is for you to fill in...

Truths about Prayer to Etch Upon Your Heart:

"And when you pray, do not be like the hypocrites, for they love to pray standing in the synagogues and on the street corners to be seen by men. I tell you the truth, they have received their reward in full. But when you pray, go into your room, close the door and pray to your Father, who is unseen. Then your Father, who sees what is done in secret, will reward you. And when you pray, do not keep on babbling like pagans, for they think they will be heard because of their many words. Do not be like them, for your Father knows what you need before you ask him." (Matthew 6:5–8)

"This, then, is how you should pray: 'Our Father in heaven, hallowed be your name, your kingdom come, your will be done, on earth as it is in heaven. Give us to-day our daily bread. Forgive us our debts, as we also have forgiven our debtors. And lead us not into temptation, but deliver us from the evil one.'" (Matthew 6:9–13)

"If you believe, you will receive whatever you ask for in prayer." (Matthew 21:22)

And pray in the Spirit on all occasions with all kinds of prayers and requests. With this in mind, be alert and always keep on praying for all the saints. (Ephesians 6:18)

Do not be anxious about anything, but in everything, by prayer and petition, with thanksgiving, present your requests to God. And the peace of God, which transcends all understanding, will guard your hearts and your minds in Christ Jesus. (Philippians 4:6–7)

Devote yourselves to prayer, being watchful and thankful. (Colossians 4:2)

Let us then approach the throne of grace with confidence, so that we may receive mercy and find grace to help us in our time of need. (Hebrews 4:16)

Be joyful in hope, patient in affliction, faithful in prayer. (Romans 12:12)

chapter seven

faithfulness

I remember my affliction and my wandering,
the bitterness and the gall. I well remember
them, and my soul is downcast within me.
Yet this I call to mind and therefore I have
hope: Because of the LORD's great love we are
not consumed, for his compassions never fail.
They are new every morning; great is your
faithfulness. I say to myself, "The LORD is my
portion; therefore I will wait for him."

Lamentations 3:19–24

What's wrong, Mommy? Everything's going to be okay, right, Mommy?"

As my four-year-old daughter, Erin, put her arms around me and hugged me, tears continued to flow.

I have to be strong. Pull yourself together, Jill. You need to be strong for Erin. The sound of my aunt and uncle approaching roused me to compose myself. It was obvious that I'd been crying, so they probed in their caring way. "Jill, what's wrong?"

Without hesitation, the floodgates burst open and I poured out everything I had kept bottled up for so long. "I don't want Hunter to die," I sobbed. "Why does he have to suffer so much? Why won't God heal him? I don't understand all this God stuff. If Hunter's going to heaven, I want to go too. I want to be there." As I continued to ramble on in desperation, Erin stood next to me and held my hand. I should have sheltered her from my meltdown—but I didn't.

I was frantic. I wanted hope and heaven. I was tired of running; the anguish of searching had wiped me out. When I finally stopped to breathe, Jim and Patsy motioned for me to come into the living room. "Let's just pray right now. Jill, God knows what you need," they said. "You need Him. You need Jesus."

I dropped to my knees, and as we knelt down to pray, I looked at Erin. She was crying too. The look on her face broke my heart. Knowing that I wouldn't have the slightest idea what to pray, Uncle Jim told me to repeat after him, and so I did . . .

~

I don't remember the exact words I prayed that afternoon. But I remember how I felt. It was real, and I'll never forget it.

When Hunter was a baby, the winter months were horrible for him because he was easily susceptible to nasty viruses. So we would pack up our entire family and head to South Florida for most of the season. My uncle Jim and aunt Patsy lived in Fort Myers, Florida, and did all the house-rental legwork for us.

Like Uncle Mark, Jim and Patsy were Christians. Upon returning to their home one afternoon after house hunting, I started sobbing. I think the weight of everything was wearing me down and I just had to let go.

Now, as I vividly recall those moments on my knees crying out to God, I realize with even greater conviction what I couldn't possibly have understood then. It wasn't about how or what I prayed—as if spew-

ing "magical," spiritual-sounding words could make any difference at all.
It wasn't about my desperation or need for hope. It wasn't even about
acknowledging my sin and repenting, because I didn't understand the
breadth of my sin at the time or what godly repentance was. Nothing
I did or didn't do could possibly have altered the course of my life
and eternity. I could barely function enough to make sense of the most
meaningless of tasks—I was a complete wreck.

It was just Jesus; what He did in the power of God's love and faithfulness working through Him to save me—to save our entire family.

Just Jesus.

Of all the moments etched into my life that I've shared thus far, this
defining moment was the most significant; changing the trajectory of my
life forever. Certainly the other moments that led up to this were vi-
tal and very much a part of the journey to bring me to my knees. But
this one solitary watershed moment changed me, and my remaining moments, forever.

Like the verse in the beginning of this chapter, I remember my affliction and can still feel the unforgiving pain of watching my one and
only son suffer every day of his life. The despair that brought me to my
knees in desperation; the suffering that exposed our weaknesses and His
strength; the heart-wrenching agony that brought us to the foot of the
cross—where life surrendered to death, that in dying, we might live.

I didn't discover Him in religion.

I didn't find Him in the false hope the world offers.

As strange and even offensive as it may seem, I caught a glimpse of
the Father's faithfulness in the midst of my son's suffering—because His
Son suffered.

⌒

"You look so beautiful, Erin," I whispered.

Dressed in all white to reflect the deeper meaning of the

monumental occasion, Erin was glowing in a way I had never witnessed before. I hugged her tightly one last time, then ran over to where the iPod player was in the back right corner of the room.

As she stood hand in hand with her dad in the back of the small prayer chapel, Pastor Rich looked my way and gave me a nod.

I pressed play and the lyrics from Tim McGraw's "My Little Girl" began to fill the room.

Jim and Erin walked arm in arm toward the altar in the front of the chapel while the song continued to play. It took everything in me not to completely fall apart. When they reached Pastor Rich at the altar, I turned down the music and made my way to the front pew where Camryn and my parents were seated. There was a stillness and peace about the room that you could almost feel. It was as if we were about to witness a wedding. Like we were standing on holy ground about to hear the voice and heart of God.

As Erin's mother, it was way more than I could comprehend in the moment. Pastor Rich welcomed everyone and explained why we were all there. Everyone who had impacted Erin's life was seated in the front three pews in that room.

"Erin has decided to make a promise to God today. A promise that you are all about to witness. A promise that you will be accountable to help Erin keep. A promise before God and all of you to remain pure until marriage." As Pastor Rich continued, Erin was captivated. I could tell by the sweet, sincere look on her face that she was nervous yet fully committed to what she was about to do. I held back tears while Erin shared her heart's desire to commit her body, heart, and mind to purity to glorify Jesus.

God is faithful. He is. Erin making a vow before the Lord and her family to remain pure until she gets married is nothing short of the immeasurable faithfulness of God. When I was thirteen years old, I didn't even know what it meant to be pure. I didn't know that God had a perfect plan for my life that included keeping my body for the gift of marriage.

The truth had set me free. Free to share with Erin that her father and I were not pure when we got married. We didn't know God then and had no idea that we were accountable to Him. We never considered the fallout and ramifications of our self-centered choices. But He did. God took the ashes of our sinful choices and made them beautiful—He made Erin. And now Erin is His and she has chosen to commit her body and sexual purity to the Lord. He took what the enemy meant for evil and shame in our lives and made it part of His good and perfect plan.

As we celebrated Erin's thirteenth birthday and her pledge to purity that afternoon, I couldn't help but praise God for His faithfulness. I pondered over the countless times I had pleaded with Him to help me share the truth with Erin. There were photos of me at our wedding holding her. She was a smart little girl and I knew she would eventually figure it all out. It was inevitable that I would have to tell her. So I prayed about it often and asked others to pray that when God had readied her heart and mine, He would give me the perfect opportunity to tell Erin. And that He would give me the right words to share everything with her, words that would help her understand so the truth would set her free—free from what had bound me for so long.

The crazy thing is, He knew. God knew that Jim and I would make the choices we did. He had already conceived of Erin Marie and her destiny—every person and event her life would impact—before He knit her together in my womb. And He knew that He would take the ashes of our choices and redeem and restore us—all of us, including Erin, back to Himself. He would make something more beautiful than we could conceive or imagine. He would first rescue us from ourselves; the flesh and sin nature that He died to save us from. But then He would also allow Erin to be the radiance of His faithfulness through her decision to not do what her parents did in their rebellion and ignorance.

You see, it's not that I was ashamed or concerned how she might react when I would eventually tell her. The Lord had given me the peace that passes understanding with respect to what the outcome of our conversation would be. I was certain even before I told her that everything would be fine. I suppose my fear in telling her circles back to that beautiful September day when I was walking home from school. The day I stood on the cracked sidewalk, stunned by words spoken from a friend. The moment when I found out that my mother was pregnant with me *before* she was married. The learning curve of my understanding of love and its meaning changed that day. I was worried that this very thing might happen to my daughter. Yes, she needed to know the truth, but I prayed and hoped that the Truth would set her free rather than enslave her to lies, like it did me. What would keep her from a heart hardened by lies from the enemy of her soul? God's faithfulness. Love and truth would protect Erin.

It did and still does.

Much of who we are is learned through living in our families. In other words, the "do as I say and not as I do" card some parents play may spin well, but it doesn't produce a winning hand for the next generation in real life. The way we live our values, habits, conduct, and such tends to be forged through emulating our parents. For example, a diligent, hardworking honest father sets an example his children will ultimately follow. Conversely, an irresponsible couch potato will shape that same sort of person. The principle tends to apply across the board. For example, alcoholic parents tend to produce children that drink and parents who attend church regularly often find that their children grow up and become consistently involved in church.

In this particular case, my family seemed to have created a pattern of premarital sex and even pregnancy that was passed from generation to generation. It was more like bondage that we didn't know how to break. However, I believe with all my heart that the generational bondage to this specific sin has been broken for our family. By this I certainly don't mean that our family and the generations to come in our lineage will no longer sin. What God's faithfulness has done as a result of Erin's commitment has taken the decisions that have been made apart from God concerning premarital sex (in my relationship, my parents' relationship, and my mother's parents' relationship) and rescued Erin (and Camryn) from its perpetuation. What has been is *not* what will be! He has used our choices and His forgiveness and the redemption of them to reveal the truth to Erin—the more perfect ways of God through His Son, Jesus.

I'm not naive enough to think the temptation will no longer be there for our girls. Of course they will be tempted, and maybe with even greater vigor because of the commitment to purity that's been made. Neither of them is married yet, so the verdict is still out. Or is it? Regardless, I'm convinced that God will continue to be faithful, because that's who He is and He'll never change. Despite the depth of my faith or that of my daughters, God will always and forever be faithful.

⌒

It was a typical winter day. The road was covered with ice and snow was falling faster than my windshield wipers could push it away. As I slowly made my way to my friend's house, I contemplated what I would say to this shattered woman I had never even met. I thought about all that Jim and I had been through and how God had restored what the enemy stole from us for so many years. I wondered how I would share the depth of what God had done in the midst of so much heartbreak. I had never revealed this part of our story to anyone, and the book containing this amazing portion of our testimony had yet to be published. I was hesitant, even somewhat reluctant, and wondered why I had agreed to the meeting. When I finally arrived I sat in the truck and said a quick prayer before I went in the house.

"Hey, Jill. I'm glad you made it. I can't believe how bad it is outside. How are the roads?" LaDonna asked as she greeted me with a hug.

As I took off my boots LaDonna's friend Kristin made her way over to where we were standing. Her face told the story better than she could ever explain it, though she soon would. It didn't take much to see that waves of anguish were trying to sweep her into an abyss of deep darkness. I understood completely. After a quick introduction, we made our way into the living room and sat down.

I listened to Kristin as her all-too-familiar story poured from her trembling lips, and I prayed silently to myself. "Lord, please give me the words. Share your hope and comfort through me."

"I don't know what to do. I can't even look at my husband. He makes me sick. How did you forgive Jim? How did you trust him again?" she pleaded with desperation.

Before I can even fumble for the words, Kristin continued to pour out her shock and sorrow. "I'm sick to my stomach. I can't sleep. I'm a complete mess. I can't think straight because I keep playing this nightmare over and over again in my mind. How I found out. The other woman. I can't stop thinking about it. How did you get beyond the initial shock? How did you move past the pain? I can't do this. I can't. I just can't. And why should I?"

As she grabbed a bundle of tissues, I gently but firmly shared my story with the desperate stranger. Telling her of

God's forgiveness and how I came to discover it through my own unforgiveness and heartbreak, I explained how it's possible to forgive and even forget.

She listened, staring at me in disbelief, unable to see past the hurt that was completely justified. She couldn't understand this kind of forgiveness and love because she didn't know the One who makes all things new, including ruined marriages, broken hearts, and crushed dreams.

"I just don't understand. I don't see how this can ever get better. How am I ever going to forgive him?"

Her pain reminded me of my own. I remember feeling as if there were no way out, that divorce was inevitable. And yet, the inevitable didn't happen. Instead, we were changed when God resurrected our dead relationship. If He did this for us—certainly He would do it for Kristin and Rob.

"Thank God our two kids are young enough. They have no idea what's going on right now. Even if we end up staying together, I just don't know how I'm ever going to trust him again." She cried out in frustration and anger as tears flowed freely down her cheeks. "I can't imagine letting him touch me ever again. Ugh, why did he have to do this? How is this ever going to get better?"

Before she can say another word I began to share and as I did, it felt as if the heart of God reached into the moment. It was like a new wave of healing was restoring my soul again, revealing His faithfulness afresh to me. "Kristin, forgiveness and healing are impossible without God. I can sit here and tell you that I love Jim more now than I ever have only because God reached in and rescued us in every way. And for me to be able to share my pain with you, knowing that I've been where you are and felt how you feel right now, it's only God. There is no other way. It has to be . . ."

"But how? How do I get where you are right now?" she anxiously interrupts, beginning to sob.

I shared awhile longer, pointing her to the only One who is equal to her heartbreak, who can take the pieces of their lives and make something beautiful from them—just as He did with Jim and me. LaDonna comforted her as I did, and when I felt she had heard enough to digest, I jotted down my phone number so we could stay in touch.

We hugged and said our good-byes, and after I trudged over to the car, I let the dam break and the tears flow. I could hardly believe what I had just experienced; it felt like I had been sitting across from myself, listening to the anguish of my own heart all over again. I could almost see it all playing out; God using the comfort He had given me to comfort and restore another life and marriage, another heartbroken woman, another crumbling relationship. I prayed for Kristin; first for her heart to be opened to the greater truth that she is loved, and also that she would realize that God wanted to restore her and her husband back to Himself—and to each other.

My relationship with Kristin began not long after Jim and I had renewed our wedding vows. Driving home after our first meeting that stormy afternoon, the contrast between where I had been and where I was completely overwhelmed me as I became so aware of being lavished in God's outrageous love. I found myself reflecting on some of the events that had led up to the defining moments in my life and marriage, and how the impossible becomes possible. I couldn't help but be awestruck by how incredible it was that Jim and I had not just survived, but had begun to flourish and thrive in our relationship.

Everything had changed. Divorce was no longer lurking around the corner of our relationship. Unforgiveness and deception had no part in our marriage anymore; unconditional love had healed our broken and hardened hearts. After twelve years of marital strife, we had finally discovered what real love was. We were now truly in love, possibly for the first time ever—for real. It was incredible. It was a miracle. It was a vivid, crystal-clear picture of God's faithfulness and redemption. I was convinced that the same God could do the impossible for my new friend.

Clearly, we didn't have it all figured out then, and Jim and I are far from the picture-perfect marriage right now. We're a work in progress that needs continuous and unrelenting prayer. But here's the most important thing: we are not the same people anymore. We're banking on the faithfulness of God now and will until we see Him face to face someday. Jim and I have absolutely no desire to go back to the old life filled with darkness, lived apart from God. Our lives were so saturated with sin and self-indulgence that only a divine work of God could have rescued us—and it did. He gave us our marriage back; a commitment of love that is real, long-suffering, and everlasting—a relationship better than it ever was, stronger than it ever could have been. Because He's faithful, even when we're not.

In all this I can't help but remember in the most profound way that God never gave up on my marriage and never will. Though my husband and I have been through so much, literally from the day we met until now, God was and still is sovereign and good. During those moments that I sat listening to Kristin pour out the depth of her sorrow and pain, I knew that God would be faithful once again. Faithful not only to her, but to me as well, to use the comfort that He had given me to comfort someone else with the light of His love as they wandered hopelessly through their valley of the shadow of death. It was almost as if everything was coming around full circle.

I'm reminded even as I write this that the Lord isn't finished with me yet. He's not finished with my husband, our marriage, or our family. He's not finished with Kristin and Rob and their marriage. He's not finished with you either. God's commitment is governed by His character. Thus His fidelity to our highest good remains unmovable whether we lead victorious or defeated lives. He will love us in the valleys as much as on the mountaintops. And in His faithfulness, He will complete the work He has begun.

"'I am the LORD, the God of all mankind. Is anything too hard for me?'" (Jer. 32:27). For so long as I struggled for years through the perils of marriage, I was convinced that staying with Jim was an impossible feat, far beyond my ability to endure. And yet in my weaknesses His presence, grace, and power proved sufficient—I'm still married and happier than I've ever been.

"And we know that in all things God works for the good of those who love him, who have been called according to his purpose" (Rom. 8:28). I never thought anything good would actually come from the heart-wrenching marital strife Jim and I endured. Certainly I never imagined that having a terminally ill son would ever prove to be "good." Yet even now, the Lord continues to show me daily how He has used sickness, death, depression, fear, anxiety, suffering, and so much more of what hurt so deeply for good. My meeting and friendship with Kristin is a perfect example. It was our mutual pain that brought us together. Had I not experienced what I did, I would not have had anything to offer her; no comfort to share, no greater hope of restoration, and no joy despite the suffering. God continues to be faithful to use the very things that hurt the most to reveal more of Himself to me—to heal me, to change me, and to ultimately set me free to love more. The more I surrender and allow Him to use my pain, the more I see the amazing way He *works all things together for good.* In His faithfulness, He used my tears to put a smile on a hurting woman's face, bringing His glory and comfort to someone who needed Him most through my heartbreak—it's crazy. But I'm living it every day. And He continues to reveal to me how our marriage and love is part of His greater purpose and plan to help marriages in peril and those on the brink of divorce.

"'For I know the plans I have for you, declares the LORD, plans to prosper you and not to harm you, plans to give you hope and a future'" (Jer. 29:11). His plans for me, for Jim, for our children, and for you—are good. God is for us! When it appeared that all hope was gone, it was because appearances are deceiving—not because hope had forsaken us. God hadn't dozed off on His throne, ducked out to play a practical joke on one of the seraphim, or left Gabriel in charge while He ran to McDonald's for a Big Mac and a Diet Coke! The greatest Love ever known was so committed to our marriage that He filled our lives with a love we had never known—apart from Him. A love deeper than our pain. A passionate love that never fails. He has proven time and time again in ways we never could have imagined, and through fiery trials we never could have endured, that He is more than enough.

So often I had put expectations on Jim that he was never able to fulfill, nor was he meant to. I needed to trust that God would meet all my needs according to His glorious riches in Christ Jesus (see Phil. 4:19). I learned that truly He is the only one capable of fulfilling our deepest desires. What a relief it is to know that I can let my husband off the hook. And in letting him off the hook, it frees me to love him exactly for who he is and where he's at right now—just as God does.

"Being confident of this, that he who began a good work in you will carry it on to completion until the day of Christ Jesus" (Phil. 1:6). Letting God do what *only He can do* is liberating. The work He began is *His* work that *He* has promised to complete. As we seek to know and love Him more (which is a work of God in and of itself), He continues to show us that we really can cast all our cares upon Him because He cares for us; deeply, intimately—in every way. And as we learn through experience that we're in better hands when we're in His hands, mountains move and we are changed. When we back off and allow Him back on to the throne of our hearts, the impossible becomes possible.

The journey of becoming more and more like Christ isn't easy. In fact, He promised we would have trials but He also promised to be with us—

no matter what. I'm comforted in knowing that just as I am a work in progress, so is my husband, and so is our marriage. Our messiness and neediness make God's grace all the more outrageous and profound. It moves our hearts to expose the depth of our need so that people like Kristin might reach out and perhaps find empathy and hope in the midst of their circumstances. Surrendering to the Lord doesn't mean that our circumstances change overnight, but our attitude and the way we relate to them often does. Knowing that He is always at work gives me the confidence to see every breath for the gift it is and live more gratefully because He's faithful.

And as the incredible story goes, Kristin began to attend my Bible study and surrendered her life to Christ, every jagged piece of it. It wasn't long before she and Rob began to go to church and marriage counseling. The net effect of their efforts was that Kristin and Rob renewed their wedding vows and are moving forward in the love of God, more in love with each other than ever. Have they "arrived"? Of course not. Who does this side of eternity? But they're healed and headed in the right direction, because in the midst of their marital strife Jesus took hold of their hearts and brought them to the only place where healing and restoration can be found. They recognized that the mountain they faced would be impossible to climb with their natural abilities even on their best day. The strength, restoration, and healing they needed would only be found in a relationship with the One that holds all things together— their Savior. They found Christ together, and as a result He saved their marriage and family. And as I write this they're expecting their fourth child. God is faithful!

I think this verse shares exactly what God did:

> Praise be to the God and Father of our Lord Jesus Christ, the Father of compassion and the God of all comfort, who comforts us in all our troubles, so that we can comfort those in any trouble with the comfort we ourselves have

received from God. For just as the sufferings of Christ flow over into our lives, so also through Christ our comfort overflows. If we are distressed, it is for your comfort and salvation; if we are comforted, it is for your comfort, which produces in you patient endurance of the same sufferings we suffer. And our hope for you is firm, because we know that just as you share in our sufferings, so also you share in our comfort. (2 Corinthians 1:3–7)

I pray you'll remember that God hasn't given up on you, or the circumstances that weigh heavily upon your heart right now. No matter how bad or hopeless things appear, cling to the reality that God cannot be shaken. He's the strong knot at the end of your rope, holding everything together. His plans for your life are good, immeasurably more than all you could ask or imagine. The Lord is still the Author and Giver of all good things. Our circumstances may be greater than we are, but God is greater than they are, no matter how daunting they may be. Our lives are safe and secure, held close in the depths of His gracious heart. Now *that's* good news!

⌒

The sound of Jim practicing his turkey calls echoes through the kitchen. It's hunting season, and his excitement will not be contained. "Hey, Zac's going to sleep over tonight so we can go hunting over at George's tomorrow morning, okay?" Jim asks as he lays his camo jacket on top of the table near where I'm sitting.

"Of course, that sounds like fun. When's he coming over?"

"He'll be here soon. He's so excited, Jill. I hope we at least see something tomorrow," Jim says as he walks into the living room.

Zac arrives late so we don't have much time to talk before Jim says it's time for bed. He's growing into a fine young man and I can't help but think of Hunter whenever I'm around him. Zac was born eleven days before Hunter. Jim and his brother Danny, Zac's dad, used to talk about the boys and the fun they would have growing up together—until Hunter got sick.

Before climbing into bed, I realize that I'd left the book I'm reading in the front room, so I get up to get it. As I walk by the kitchen I notice that the floor is covered, so I stop to see what the mess is all about. There in the middle of the kitchen floor are two hunting outfits lying side by side. One for Jim and the other for our nephew Zac.

I kneel down on top of the camo outfits and start bawling uncontrollably. "This should be Hunter's hunting outfit. Why can't he be the one going hunting with Daddy?" I cry out. I get up and walk into the living room nearby and try to compose myself. I'm thankful the girls and Jim and Zac are sleeping so I don't have to explain my tears. For the first time I feel like God has allowed me to experience the pain and anguish of what missing Hunter might be like for Jim.

And yet God whispers, "But I gave him another hunting buddy." Who knew that Zac would love hunting? Who could have anticipated that he would long to spend hours in the woods with Uncle Jim?

Later that afternoon they return with one of the biggest turkeys Jim said he had ever laid eyes on. Zac's first hunt is a huge hit. The smile on his face is beaming like a neon success story.

⌒

It fits like the pieces of the puzzle life so often is: God being faithful to pour his goodness through the land of the living, a father's heart to hunt with his son, God blessing Jim with Zac, and Zac with Jim, and God allowing me to experience grief for Jim when I couldn't for so long because I was so caught up in my own sorrow.

And yet in the throes of that sorrow, like a light piercing the shadows it cast across my heart and my hope, God's faithfulness allowed me to see grace in the moment that was greater than our loss, because He's God and He knows the plans He has for us. They are good, bringing hope and a future, inspiring us to press on in the promise of a relationship that will be reunited someday.

Before God opened my heart to be filled with something greater than my loss, I could only see what we were missing rather than what God was trying to give to us. For a long time it had been very difficult for me to be around Zac because I saw him through our loss. Suddenly I was able to see him through the eyes of God and realized that we had found a treasure greater than gold in him. We weren't playing "catch-up football" anymore—the momentum had shifted and it was a whole new ball game!

⌒

"I can't believe he's gone," Jim said and sighed deeply as he looked out the truck window. It was a beautiful Mississippi morning. The warmth of the sun filled the truck as we drove to the cemetery for Kent's burial service.

Trying to comfort Jim, I started talking about what the preacher said at church. "Did you know that Kent was doing prison ministry and attending Bible study weekly for years?" I asked.

"I knew he was doing something with prisons but I had no idea what. And no, we never talked about Bible study and stuff like that."

A deep sigh forced back tears longing to break out and I could tell that Jim was holding back. He wanted to cry but didn't.

"That's my boy," he said as we continued to drive. The line of cars stretched for miles. Everybody loved Kent Hull. Friends, family, and the beloved Buffalo Bills football family had flown in from all over the country.

Making the turn into the cemetery, we pulled over and parked, waiting in the car while the family gathered near the casket. As we moved in close to hear the preacher share a closing verse, I noticed the men in green waiting. Just behind the preacher, separated by a twelve-foot-tall wire fence, I saw them. Both with shovel in hand, waiting. Waiting patiently to pile dirt back on. Waiting to do their job. Bury bodies of loved ones. Cover the tears cried over caskets. Smooth dirt over broken lives and hearts. Why did they have to stand right there? Their presence is insensitive, careless, and it unnerves me. They don't even know Kent. Can't they wait somewhere else? Can't they at least put their shovels down so it's not so obvious that they're waiting for the end?

"And this is not the end—it's just the beginning for Kent," the preacher said, continuing to share encouragement from God's Word. Scriptures filled with eternal hope that I believed with all my heart to be true. Words that I had been clinging to since my last graveside experience. Even as my heart filled with assurance from the truth being spoken, I was distracted. Frustrated by their waiting, I moved back behind Jim so I didn't have to look at them any longer.

But the pain of remembering moved with me. I began to feel that familiar ache pressing deep into my heart as tears made a trail down my cheeks. The memory of that beautiful day was so vivid and real. I see the white chairs and the fake green grass where everyone has gathered around the boy's hunter-green casket. I can smell the aroma of the bundles of white roses covering and cascading down off the metal box that holds his precious, frail, eight-year-old body. I hear the words from Scripture welling up in my heart and pouring out of my mouth. "Therefore, if anyone is in Christ, he is a new creation; the old has gone, the new has come" (2 Cor. 5:17).

I close my eyes for a moment and remember the small white pieces of paper, filled with life, longing to burst forth, folded in a triangle with special dates printed on the front: HUNTER JAMES KELLY, FEBRUARY 14, 1997–AUGUST 5, 2005. I unfold the memory in my heart and watch as my sweet baby girl, Camryn, opens her special white triangle and out bursts life that was hidden within the paper. Butterflies are everywhere. Beauty flutters all around us. Life has come to our moment of death. For a moment I am swept up in the greater reality—Hunter is alive in heaven with Jesus. Though death has come to his body, new life is his forever, and it's mine forever too. The boy is in my future. Jesus made this possible. My momentary burst of joy is soon shrouded in grief. The thought of the pile of dirt waiting nearby to cover my only son crashes the party and I am upset again. How I longed to dig up the dirt just to touch and hold him one more time.

When the preacher finished, he told us we could pay our respects to Kent's family. And so we did. We made our way over to the yawning gash in the earth that patiently waited for the body of Jim's best friend. And as we waited our turn to hug and say good-bye to the children and wife left behind, the men in green waited too . . . Waited and watched.

There were hundreds of people and the line was long. After we walked away, Jim stopped to talk to some of his fellow teammates while I continued on toward our truck. Flooded with emotion, I tried to hide my tears by ducking away from the crowd. I just wanted to be alone. I wanted to think and pray. My friend Patti motioned for me to come over and sit with her in her vehicle, so I swung the front driver's side door of the car open and sat down.

"I just can't believe he's gone," she says with a deep sigh from the backseat of the car.

"I know," I responded, turning to look out the front window.

And just then, in that very moment, a huge, beautiful monarch butterfly landed on the hood of the car near the windshield, right in front of where I sat.

"I can't believe it! I can't believe it," I whispered to myself, shaking my head. "There's a butterfly. Right here, right now. Out of nowhere, there's a butterfly." I continued to celebrate the unexpected blessing of the moment.

⌒

A butterfly. I felt like God was reaching into the moment to rescue my heart. To remind me of the wonders He had done and the hope of what's to come. A blessed assurance that all I believed in that moment was true. These moments in time etched upon our hearts, they hurt down deep, yet in the pain a greater hope and resolve is birthed. For there's more to the story, to His story—this is not the end. There's a reminder of new life now and the hope of what's to come, as if eternity and the hope of forever lies tucked between the lines of life. No, this is not the end of the story, not for Kent, not for Hunter, not for any of us who call on His Name. And because this is not the end, coming to the end of ourselves and actually dying so that we might live is the only way to live.

Some may be tempted to view the butterfly connection between Hunter's and Kent's passing as coincidence, maybe superstition, or even overspiritualizing—but I don't think so. I won't deny that the events demand a measure of faith to see their relationship to one another and, more important, to God, but through the eyes of faith I see it . . . and in seeing it, my heart soars like a butterfly borne aloft, rising with hope and lighting peacefully upon the promises of God.

⌒

"They're out there strutting," Jim yells to me from the kitchen.

I shake my head, smile, and continue writing.

The door to the office swings open.

"Hey—do you know where my binos are? I can't find them. The turkeys are back. Did you see them?" he interrupts. I leave the writing and go to the window with Jim. Sometimes I need his inconvenient interruptions.

There are twenty-three turkeys in our backyard. It's the middle of winter and they're hungry. While the hens dig for food, a few of the toms bust out in full strut; they're trying to show off for the ladies.

My turkey gazing ends with a loud vibration from my iPhone. I walk back over to my desk, sit down, and grab my phone. It's a text from my dear friend Katie. Immediately I read it; hoping everything is okay with Karis, Katie's daughter. She has Krabbe disease, like Hunter did, so Katie and I have a very special friendship. God has allowed our paths to cross because of our deepest heartbreak and joy—the suffering of our children and our love for the suffering Savior.

The text message was actually a follow-up to a text conversation we had had the day before while I was sequestered at the lodge fasting and praying.

Katie: The urologist couldn't find a reason for Karis not uri-nating. They said sometimes this happens even in healthy kids. We just have to pray for her to start going again. Until then, we have to use the catheter.

Me: My friend, I will pray. I'm in a time of prayer and fasting. And I will talk to Jesus for my friend whom I love...the sweet one He loves.

Katie: Thank you, Jill. I've noticed that powerful things happen when I fast. I will pray that He gives you more of Himself during this time.

Me: Amen! Thank you. He has. I'm writing and He is just wrecking me! But it's good, because He is! I love you so much!

I remember praying for Karis at the lodge in the mid-dle of my writing (the chapter on prayer). "Lord, PLEASE! Help her pee! Open the floodgates and let it all out, Father. Please! You know her frail little body more than anyone. You know her. You know exactly what she needs. You know she needs to go potty. PLEASE DO SOMETHING!"

The next text I received from Katie was the mes-sage that dropped in as I was watching the turkeys in our backyard with Jim.

Katie: Remember what I said yesterday about the crazy things I've seen when God's children fast? Karis wet her diaper last night. First time in almost two weeks. No rea-son...just Jesus. Hope your faith is strengthened.

I put my phone down and started celebrating.

A miracle. A moment of faithfulness fulfilled. A prayer answered! I was only responding to texts and calls that were necessary during my prayer time at the lodge. Could you imagine if I had missed Katie's text? What if I had gotten so caught up in what I had to do that I missed out on praying for Karis?

I would've missed this display of God's splendor.

I would've missed the moment.

I would've missed Him.

So this has me thinking. God answers prayer—because it's all about Him and His perfect plan, right? And He is faithful to Himself—as far as who He is and the promises He has made. He is faithful. He is. But what if we miss out on receiving the blessing of His faithfulness and goodness in action because we're caught up in our own little worlds and circumstances in life? Maybe that explains what I like to call divine intrusions, or the whole compendium of ways that God uses circumstances like a stone in our shoe or speck in our eye—or a mark on our arm. Irritations that force us out of our comfort zones, routines, and safe havens in order to put us in a position where God can demonstrate His character and faithfulness so we learn to trust Him more.

I learn a lot about trusting God through teachings and sermons, and studying His Word. But I learn to trust God by being in a "make it or break it" position where I actually have to trust Him to come through, to be faithful to His Word, to be faithful to me. That doesn't mean that the answer to every prayer is the way I want it to go, but it does mean that He continues to love me, hear me, and pursue my highest good in His love and faithfulness. And *that*, I can live with ... forever!

When I think of my relationship with God, I think a lot about faith because Hebrews 11:6 declares, "And without faith it is impossible to please God, because anyone who comes to him must believe that he exists and that he rewards those who earnestly seek him." There it is, without faith it is impossible to please God, end of story, do not pass Go, do not collect $200! In fact, the entire eleventh chapter is about the importance of faith and what a believer can accomplish through believing. However, like all things biblical, it's easy to cut and paste and only heed the parts of Scripture that fit our agendas and circumstances.

Take Hebrews 11:6 for example. The second part of it has a lot to say: "Anyone who comes to him must believe that he exists and that he rewards those who earnestly seek him." It holds the mystery of the relationship between faith and faithfulness; we must believe that He is, and that in His faithfulness He will reward us as we earnestly seek Him. But look, He's all about relationship; "earnestly seek Him," *not* earnestly seek what He can do for you!

Faithfulness on our part implies our believing in the face of circumstances and events that would appear to deny the love of God, the faithfulness of God, the justice of God, and so on. My point, my friend, is that faithfulness is expressed and exercised in contrast, or when its leaned against. Consider marriage, for example, remaining faithful to our vows is a non-issue until temptation strikes and gives us something to be faithful in the face of. In nature, if a butterfly is helped from its cocoon instead of fighting its way through it, it will never fly. That's because it's the opposition it faces while struggling to break free from the cocoon that strengthens its wings enough to support flight.

Similarly, with God it's a two-edged sword, our faithfulness to Him and His to us on the same blade. The real beauty about this is that though our side of the blade may grow blunt from use and need to be sharpened from time to time, God's edge is always sharp—He always remains faithful. He is the reward of those who earnestly seek Him!

What to Remember and Never Forget...

- The Lord meets us at our level of comprehension. Understanding is critical, but offering our wounded hearts to Him in sweet surrender is not a theological exercise. If anything, it's an exercise in desperation and sheer honesty.
- Often the call to be faithful is inconvenient. It comes at very inopportune times and is usually problematic, but it results in spiritual growth, confidence in God, and a deeper love for Him—as well as deeper trust in Him.
- Faithfulness is built through trials and exercise. Like a butterfly strengthening its wings as it breaks out of its cocoon, our faithfulness is strengthened through opposition as circumstances and challenges lean against it.
- God is faithful even when we're not, and He continues to help us mature and grow in faithfulness.

Prayer...

Oh Lord, I long to be a faithful servant filled with so much love for You that I am true to You and faithful to Your Word at all times. Please fill me with the grace to be faithful no matter how inconvenient it is, how painful it may be, how difficult the road is. Forgive me when I blow it, help me rise when I fall and remain humble in the throes of success. But, Lord, even more than this please help me to always remember and never forget Your faithfulness. At all times. In every circumstance. I love you, Jesus.
~Amen!

Truths about God's Faithfulness to Etch Upon Your Heart:

For the word of the LORD is right and true; he is faithful in all he does. (Psalm 33:4)

But you, Lord, are a compassionate and gracious God, slow to anger, abounding in love and faithfulness. (Psalm 86:15)

Your kingdom is an everlasting kingdom, and your dominion endures through all generations. The LORD is faithful to all his promises and loving toward all he has made. (Psalm 145:13)

He will keep you strong to the end, so that you will be blameless on the day of our Lord Jesus Christ. God, who called you into fellowship with his Son Jesus Christ our Lord, is faithful. (1 Corinthians 1:8–9)

But the Lord is faithful, and he will strengthen and protect you from the evil one. (2 Thessalonians 3:3)

chapter eight

death

My face pressed up against the kitchen window as I watched my dad dig a hole near the hillside to the left side of our home. Tears poured down my cheeks faster than I could wipe them away.

Our beloved dog Bowser was dead.

He'd been missing for a few days, and my brother, Jack, finally found him lying lifeless in the small creek near the bottom of our driveway. We were so sad; he was such a good dog. A cocker spaniel/golden retriever mix with lots of spunk and love. We had just moved from the village out to the country when Bowser got loose. And though we searched and waited for his return, he never came back.

As I watched my father make ready the hole that would consume our beloved pet, my mother tried to console me. "He was such a good dog, wasn't he? Remember when..." She stopped abruptly midsentence. "Why don't we go in the other room, Jill?" She gently grabbed my arm and began to walk away. I could tell that she didn't want me to look out the window anymore. She didn't want me to see what happens when death comes. I knew she was trying to distract me, but I didn't fall for it. I turned back to look out the window just in time to see my father put the black garbage bag that held Bowser into the hole.

And then he stopped.

And cried.

His shoulders were shaking as he broke down in tears.

That was the second time I saw my dad cry.

⌒

Death comes to all of us.

We all stop breathing.

No one is exempt.

We dread death from the moment we understand what it is. It's the 5,000-pound bull elephant snorting in the middle of the living room, glaring arrogantly into your eyes. It hangs in the air like a foul stench as we all fasten our seat belts on a plane, every passenger thinking the same disturbing thought: "I hope the plane doesn't go down."

We don't want to think about it, talk about it, deal with it, or go through it. We wish it would go far, far away and never come back. Many of us spend much of our lives pretending it doesn't exist—until it barges in, summoning us to the funeral of a friend or loved one. It hurts deep and lingers long, reminding us that life is fragile and fleeting. The uneasy reality it shoves in our face is that we're not promised another day, another minute, another breath, another heartbeat. What we *are* promised is that our heart *will* stop beating—count on it.

Sometimes it comes like a thief in the night, catching us completely by surprise; mocking our sense of security and ripping the foundation we believed would bear any burden out from under us. At other times we watch it progress slowly, ebbing along as it casually sucks the life right out of us. And we stand watching, desperate, helpless to stop its fierce, unrelenting, leisurely vengeance. All the while trying to fill our lives with every possible distraction this world has to offer as the inevitable inches closer with each passing breath.

For me, death came when Bowser died. He was just a dog, but he wasn't—he was a companion, a friend, and a beloved pet. Even so, the loss of a pet doesn't remotely compare to the heartbreak and devastation of losing a family member, loved one, or friend. But any way you look at it, death is a gutless thief, intruding with stealth and stealing our greatest treasures against their will—and ours.

⌒

"It shouldn't be much longer," the doctor says as he holds Alice's frail wrist. He's counting the pulse of every heartbeat while we watch and anticipate every single breath. She inhales then exhales slowly as we cling to a mirage of false hope, believing that she'll pull through yet again, like she always does. She'll tough it out and be out of the hospital in no time. Jim's mother is stout-hearted and strong. She raised six rough and raucous Kelly boys, so this disease they call emphysema should be no match for her resilience.

The small hospital room is crowded, so the brothers take turns watching, praying, and hoping. The room next door is empty, so it has become a resting place; where we all turn for respite from this heartbreak. Some of the brothers and sisters-

in-law are sitting in the hallway, waiting for word that she's
passed. Jim's dad sits next to his bride and holds her right
hand; the pain of losing his wife is written all over his coun-
tenance. With head down, eyes glossed over with tears, his
anguish fills the silent room.

It's my turn to keep watch. I don't know what to do. I don't
really know how to pray, but I fumble through it anyway.
I'm sitting in the chair at the end of her bed. The rhythmic
sound of water bubbles from the oxygen and monitors keeps
me awake while I watch and wait. I'm acting like I've been
here before but the truth is, I'm scared. I've never watched
anyone die. As much as I love Jim's mother, deep down I'm
hoping I'm not in the room when it happens—that dreadful
moment when she breathes her last.

Jim walks into the room and over to his mother's side. He
leans over and whispers in her ear.

"Hi, Mum. We're all here for you. We love you," he says and
then walks over to where I'm sitting. I don't know what to do
or say, so I hug Jim for as long as he'll let me. The waiting
has taken its toll on him—on everyone—and because it's inevitable, you can't help but want it to be over.

An obnoxious beeping noise interrupts the moment. A
nurse rushes into the room to silence the alarm. "Her breathing has become very shallow. I'm going to turn off this alarm
because it shouldn't be long," she says softly, her voice filled
with remorse.

It shouldn't be long. That's what the doctor said too, but
it's been hours.

The brothers and their wives gather around Alice, and
we watch and wait. Her breathing changes; she inhales and
then it seems like forever before she exhales. My heart begins to race and my palms are drenched in sweat as I begin

to feel like I'm going to faint. I'm afraid to watch, so I shield myself behind Jim so I don't have to look. I contemplate how I will try to be a comfort to him when this is all said and done. His mother is dying right in front of us. This is horrible.

We continue waiting and watching. She breathes slowly, then exhales.

She breathes.

And then she's . . .

Gone.

Just like that.

She stopped breathing and she was gone. No one rushed in to try and save her.

The sound of weeping fills the room as the Kelly family begins to mourn the loss of Mum.

~

It was less than a month before our wedding when Jim's mother died. While we were planning a new life together, she was dying. And then life went on—yet it didn't, at least not the way it used to be.

Jim's mother, Alice.

Then my grandma Jean.

Death is what happens to people when they get old. You're born, you live, and then you die. While old age used to be fifty, the new old is now seventy; people are living longer as they take advantage of all the medications and treatments that preserve life. In fact, according to the Centers for Disease Control, the average life expectancy is now seventy-eight and a half years.[1] The media bombards us daily with every type of anti-wrinkle, anti-age-spot, fountain-of-youth concoction out there to stop us from growing old. And ironically, most of us actually fall for the marketing ploys, though we know it's just nonsense. Still, we want to believe we might actually be able to stop our body from aging…or at least hide the evidence. It's sad but true.

In facing death we reflect upon life, pondering how the person who died has used his or her time. What filled the space between his birth date and death date? How did she live? How did he love? Everything that matters, all that's important, becomes crystal clear after a person is gone. Why is that? Why do we wait until *then* to reflect on what's critically important *now*? Is it because we get so caught up with living? In my experience, most clichés are rooted in reality. So the idea that "you don't know what you've got until it's gone" has sharp teeth and a deep bite as we get up close and personal with death.

From experiences to possessions to relationships, we try and take as much out of life as we possibly can. And then comes retirement, which we think is the life we've been waiting for because we get to do whatever we want: move to a warmer climate and spend our remaining time searching for seashells along the tranquil seashore. Consider the folly of sweating through decades of our lives to cool off and really "live" for a few thin years. We fill our lives with stuff that ends up crowding out our capacity to fully love all that God loves, because the more you own, the more it potentially owns you.

God wants us empty for the filling of all He has promised to provide for us, for everything we need—including meaning. So when we seek after the things of this world to fill our lives with joy, hope, love, fulfillment, protection, and the list goes on and on, we end up craving more because nothing this world offers can actually fulfill us.

We're convinced that more is better, often courtesy of the media, our families, and our friends. More money, more things, more influence, more success, more everything—except the things that hurt. I don't know anyone who has longed for more pain, trials, stress, or death; the very things that commonly cause us to stop in the midst of our chaotic lives and assess our priorities. Because, let's be honest, our priorities routinely get out of whack more than we'd like to admit. I know this is not what we want to hear, but it's the very things we want less of that show us what our hearts truly yearn for more of—God. Period.

Even as followers of Christ, oftentimes we'd rather do more for God, when He'd rather we have more of Him (remember Mary and Martha). We get so caught up in the doing that we forget the *being* that enables us to do what we do from a pure heart. God is more concerned with who we are than what we do, more concerned with our character than our achievements. Godly character will necessarily lead to loving obedience, while its lack can still produce all kinds of good works with proud and self-righteous motives.

How many times have we gone through deeply spiritual motions when the cost is minimal and the net effect is to appear very spiritual? Flinging out a powerful prayer at the meeting, expanding on a biblical idea that you know is going to impress others, these things and so many more position us at the top of the Christian food chain, and yet they can be offensive to the Spirit of Truth if done with wrong motives. This "Christian version" of ourselves is as phony as a three-dollar bill, and worth about as much. God longs for us, the people He designed us to be, not cookie-cutter clones who rock an airtight facade. And if we are who God designed and called us to be, then we will do what He has designed and called us to do. I know you can relate to this on some level.

But here's the deal: there's nothing new under the sun. All the things of this world are dying right along with us. So we have a choice. Will we die right along with the world and its passing pleasures, or will we die to it and live for Him where the greater treasure is because He is our great reward? We treasure what we want most. Think about it. If you treasure love, you'll do whatever it takes to receive it. If you treasure validation and acceptance from people (and God), you'll break your back trying to please people (and God) in order to prove yourself. It's a vicious cycle. The more we treasure something, the more we spend ourselves in its pursuit.

Jesus told us, "For where your treasure is, there your heart will be also" (Matt. 6:21). And yet, God in His infinite grace has already given us everything we need for life and godliness through His Son, Jesus. Do you believe this? Do you believe that right now, this very moment, you have everything you need? Is your relationship with Christ your unrivaled treasure? He will never turn from us, yet He'll allow us to turn from Him if we choose. Turn from Him until we realize there is no greater treasure than knowing Him. And we awaken to find that we've turned *to* Him, and that's exactly where our treasure is.

⌒

"Mommy, I need you. Okay? Right now, Mama." Camryn grabbed my pants and gave them a big yank with her little hands to get my attention.

"Of course, Cam, what is it?" I responded, bending down to look her in the eyes.

"Come with me please, Mama," she insisted as she grabbed both my hands and led me into the living room.

Enthusiastically I said, "I'll be back in a minute to see how you're doing, Hunter. I'm sure Ms. Elizabeth will give you a good workout, buddy," letting Cam lead me into the living room.

I suddenly felt small and unguarded as she walked me over to her little butterfly blanket spread out neatly on the carpet. She motioned for me to sit down, so after we wiggled into a comfortable position, I took her hands, held them in mine, and looked deep into her beautiful blue eyes.

"So what do you want to tell me, Bammer?" I asked.

"Why does Hunter have to die? Why can't he stay here with us? Why can't you give him something to make him all better?" She peered intently back into my eyes. I suddenly realized that I had been unconsciously tensing up, bracing for the question as if I had known all along that it was coming. And come it did, with all the tact and tenderness of an on-rushing train. With everything in me I fought to hold back the tears that were forcing their way up from the churning well of pain deep within me.

Hunter was in the other room getting physical therapy, which was good because I didn't want him to hear my con-versation with Camryn. And I was thankful she didn't blurt out her barrage of questions in front of her brother. He was fully cognitive, very aware, and able to understand. Because of that, we avoided discussing diagnoses, things doctors say, death—we made it a practice not to talk about the unmen-tionables around Hunter. Never. Because he was living.

But Cam and I weren't around Hunter right here, right now, and she was asking a fair question—even though it had an unfair answer. "Sissy said heaven is better for Hunter. Why, Mama? Why is it better when we are here and not there?" she exclaimed, frustration punctuating every sentence.

I found myself drifting back to that gorgeous summer day when we were told that our only son would die before his second birthday. The sweet one asking me the dreaded "why" questions wasn't even born when we received the news. While a book sitting nearby momentarily distracted Camryn, I con-tinued to ponder over that day. I thought about coming home after the diagnosis to our nearly two-year-old daughter, Erin. It was almost as if I had to relive the nightmare all over again. Here I was—icy fingers of anguish tightening around my bro-ken heart as I strained to tell Camryn the same dreadful news I had struggled to share with Erin.

But how do you explain something like this to a four-year-old? A child? How do you explain what you don't understand yourself, even though you're an adult?

"Why does Hunter have to die?" Camryn was only four years old. She didn't understand. And neither did I. Why *did* Hunter have to die? Why did the doctor tell us on a beautiful summer day in 1997, *"Hunter will probably not live to see his second birthday"*? I will never forget that day and the many moments like the one I just shared. Moments that reminded me of the lingering fear that fell across my heart as the shadow of death fell across our lives. When those dreadful words were spoken on June 24, 1997 (which ironically would end up being Camryn's birthday two years later), the crushing reality of death leveled me. *"Your son has been diagnosed with a fatal genetic disease called Krabbe Leukodystrophy. There is no treatment for this disease and no cure. The average life expectancy for babies diagnosed with infantile Krabbe is fourteen months. Hunter will probably not live to see his second birthday. We can help you make your son more comfortable but—"*

But what?

What can you possibly do if there's nothing you can do to save our son? Help him die easier?

Her words tolled like a bell that no power on earth could silence, describing our beloved baby boy. His life, sure to grow faint, would slowly fade away with each passing day, each moment a gift of joy and pain. Every word she spoke pierced my heart like jagged glass, and I was scared out of my mind. Grasping at everything I knew to be true, I came up empty, fearful, and desperate. The very foundation I had rested my hopes upon was instantly demolished. Little did I know that the darkness of this dying would cast an unexpected light on a deeper reality, a truth that would rock my world in every way imaginable.

With the doctor's dismal assessment of my only son's condition, I was instantly consumed with his well-being, absorbed with every nuance of his care. Whatever preoccupation I may have had with myself at that time disappeared. Life was no longer about anything that pertained to me, because Hunter needed me—all of me. I couldn't worry about meaningless, selfish pursuits when he was fighting for life—for every single breath. Without even realizing it, I slowly began to die to my wants and desires and the empty promises of this world that had cluttered my heart and mind for so long. The worthless treasures of the celebrity life were exposed for the brittle trinkets they are, and I began to understand what was impossible for me to grasp before.

As I took on the disease that was trying to steal and kill my son, it didn't take long for me to realize that I was outgunned; helpless and without hope. There was nothing I could turn to—no weapon, no treatment, no cure; nothing to help him. Who was going to save my son? Who was going to rescue our family? Who was going to make this better? Jim and I didn't have the answers. We couldn't turn to each other for comfort or strength because life was draining out of us day after day as we struggled to survive the torment this disease had inflicted upon us. I couldn't weep with my husband. He had no idea how to comfort me when his own heart was broken beyond repair. And because I was swallowed up, engulfed in my own anguish, I never even considered the possibility that Jim might need me—because Hunter needed me.

I was spread so thin, giving everything I had for the boy and his two sisters, that I had nothing left to give my husband. Nothing, not even the love he deserved. And because I was giving out of my own strength, ability, and love, I eventually exhausted my reserves and came to the end of myself. Which is exactly where God wanted me—at the very end of myself, dying to all that I was. Because even on my best day my best efforts were pitifully lacking; I had nothing! I needed to start dying to all of it so that I would eventually seek the only life that is LIFE—Jesus. Recognizing that I was utterly helpless and stripped of a hope that was never real to begin with moved me in the direction where true hope would eventually be found. A place where death would actually empty into life. God chose to use my one and only son's death sentence to help *me* begin to die to myself.

When I began to understand, believe in, and eventually cling to the hope of heaven—and its Author—I became more willing to die to the futility of earthly things, making me all the more passionate about taking the greater message to others so they too might Live and Die! And as Jesus intervened and I began to live for Him, my focus in life became just that—life. It wasn't that I forgot the reality of Hunter's condition, but in living for Christ, Hunter's life became much more significant than the disease that was trying to steal it. There were those sorrowful moments when I would get the phone call that another child had succumbed to disease, or I would tackle tough questions like the ones from my daughter Cam, but even in the midst of those moments, through Christ, the light of life dispelled the shadow of death and despair that tried to cast themselves across our path. It wasn't as if death stopped knocking at the door, it was always there, but life somehow overcame its reality. Because in Christ, though outwardly we waste away, inwardly we're being renewed day by day, moment by moment.

Another deception we learned to die to was the lie that we can somehow control the circumstances around us—it's an illusion, a house of cards. Everything about our comfortable life was shattered. We didn't even realize how very comfortable we were until there was no longer a foundation to stand upon. We had no idea we idolized our comfort until we tried controlling everything under the sun in order to keep it. Ugh, this was such a dreadfully hard lesson for me to learn and eventually embrace, but God was faithful. He promised to comfort the afflicted, but in His love He also afflicts the comfortable—that they might see this life for what it truly is.

Our hope is in nothing but the Lord, who heals, binds up, and wrestles right along with us. I would often have to remind myself that Jesus knew Hunter's pain, that He felt every bit of it on the cross. And if He knew—that's all I needed to know, because trying to understand the battle my son had to endure tore me to pieces. Maybe I needed to die to myself first and foremost, but it didn't end there. I also had to die to the idea that I had some sort of control; a superior perspective as Hunter's

mother that resulted in my knowing what was best for him better than
God did. And as I did die to these illusions, I realized I could trust Him
with what I didn't know because HE KNEW. This kept me going, pressing on and into all that God had for us in the midst of the moments.

~

"You go ahead, Erin. We'll meet you in the gym," I said as we
all piled out of the truck. The school parking lot was full of
cars for the sports awards banquet. Erin ran ahead of us while
Jim and I waited patiently for Camryn to gather her things
from the backseat. She's always toting around goodies, and
we're always waiting for her.

"She had such a great season, didn't she?" I commented
about our daughter's success as we walked into the school.

"Yeah, I know, but she's still got a lot to learn," Jim responded.

The ceremony was just getting started, so we climbed half-
way up the bleachers and found a seat. I turned around to
say something to Cam but she was already gone, giggling with
some of her friends off in the corner of the gymnasium. After
what seemed like too long and many awards later, it was time
for Erin's basketball team to take the court. While the girls
lined up next to each other, Jim leaned over toward me. "I'm
going to go down there and say something," he whispered in
my ear.

Taken aback by his boldness, I turned toward him and shot
him a look. I didn't want to miss out on what Coach Sam was
saying, so I just shook my head and rolled my eyes. He wasn't
asked to say anything, so why would he? Here we go again,
the worldly "it's all about me" motivational speech.

It's not about all that.

It's not about you.

It's about honoring God.

Playing for Him and not for the recognition and accolades of this world, I complained to myself silently.

When the coach was almost finished, Jim made his way down the bleachers and onto the court. I was frustrated and embarrassed, with a look on my face that told the story of my heart at a glance.

As Jim took the microphone it was as if God gently leaned into the moment, took hold of my face, and said, "Jill, I love him just the way he is. And you need to too." Overwhelmed by His tender yet poignant conviction, I immediately put my head down and started to pray. "Lord, please forgive me and help me to love like You do. Help me to love Jim. I don't know how."

~

An understanding of the context would help in explaining why this meltdown in the bleachers was a defining, monumental moment for me. You see, for a long time I thought that Jim and I were destined for divorce, it appeared to be our only option. Deceived and convinced—I was sold, a disciple of divorce, believing it was only a matter of time. After our son, Hunter, the child I had hoped would draw Jim back to me, went to heaven, the lynchpin that held us together was gone. Divorce wasn't an option while our son battled for every breath. To break open and bleed out the wound of our languishing marriage while we were still fighting for the boy made no sense.

But he left.

Now it was just us: Jim, me, and the girls. So, given the nightmare our dream had become, I thought, Well, I must stay for them, not for any other reason but for our daughters. Staying in a marriage for any other reason but the truth that "what God has joined together, let no man sep-arate" (Matt. 19:6) is nothing more than bowing in homage to the lie that God really doesn't know what's best for us. The longing for some-one other than who God had given me was the bigger crisis. I desired the man of my dreams rather than the one God created and ordained for me, committing adultery of the heart as I longed for the grass that was greener on the other side. It was just one more way I called Him Lord, but treated Him like He was my servant.

I expected so much from Jim, and piled expectations on him that only God was meant to fulfill. Selfishly, I was living as though I somehow deserved more, better—selling myself in the most spiritual language I knew. I needed to die to my expectations of what I thought Jim was sup-posed to be. More than that, I needed to die and abandon the notion that I deserved more, better.

God changed my life that moment in the gymnasium when He spoke to me so tenderly, "Jill, I love him right now just the way he is. And you need to too." I took a step closer, redefined by the selfless love of God, and began a transformation, a new way of thinking and living that, to this very day, continues to enrich both me and those I love. When I fall, like we always do, I come back to this moment in the school gymna-sium and remind myself, so I can die again. Die to myself and live unto Christ—be more, be better for Jesus, for Jim, for my kids.

In my experience, temptation is usually a lie draped in truth, enticing us to believe that satisfaction is found in having more, doing better, or trying harder—some promising spinoff of human effort. The truth is that God alone is sufficient. He is all we need, and the only One capable of filling the human heart. Heaping expectations on other people like your husband, your children, friends, or anyone else, is sheer folly be-cause we just spin our wheels. It is nothing short of falling into the trap of believing not only that you need something more to be whole, but that something other than the God who is love can bring fulfillment. It's a lie and we need to die to this idea that we need God plus something.

The truth gets wickedly twisted, and somehow we believe that God is not sufficient or that we need God plus something in order to make our lives complete.

If you can reduce meaning, fulfillment, and true success to a not-so-secret mathematical formula, it's simply this: *Jesus plus nothing equals everything!*

⌒

"Jill, are you okay?" my mother asked, slipping her arm firmly around me.

It was as if I were in another world, completely detached from reality. The music was loud and there were people celebrating, laughing, and enjoying conversation all around me—but everything sounded muffled and distant.

"Mommy, can we please bid on the puppy? Mommy, please can we get the puppy?" Erin and Camryn tugged at my arm as the cutest, fuzziest little puppy was being passed around.

"You'll have to ask your daddy," I responded robotically, without even looking up at the girls.

"Girls, you have no way to get the puppy home. I don't think Daddy will say yes but you can ask him," Mother chimed in. "I'll help the girls find Jim so they can ask about the puppy. I'll be right back. Are you going to be okay?" she said with concern, standing up and motioning for Erin and Camryn to join her.

As she melted into the bustling crowd with the girls, a man wandered purposefully over to where I was sitting. Guarded but pleasant, I made every effort to be polite to the stranger, hearing his words leap from his heart but fall flat before I could welcome them into mine. I heard him talking but I wasn't listening. I wanted to but...I couldn't.

"Mrs. Kelly, I just wanted to tell you how sorry I am about your son, Hunter. I can't even imagine what you must be going through. I hope you raise a ton of money tonight for Hunter's Hope." It was a voice. A voice crying in the wilderness—my wilderness. Deep within, somewhere beyond this place of sorrow, I was whole, I was Jill, and though in this moment I was far away, I knew by faith that hope was around the bend. As the man continued to share, I looked to see where my mom and daughters were. I was sincerely grateful for all the support overflowing from compassionate and generous people who wanted to make a difference like we did.

Unfortunately, I was still so raw and shattered that I found myself numb—on autopilot, mechanically going through the motions just to endure an event I longed to enjoy but couldn't. I ached to express our gratitude to the countless beautiful people who had joined hands and hearts with us—it was just too soon and too hard. Thankfully, I remembered to thank him before he graciously walked away with understanding eyes.

"It's time for us to start tonight's program, so can you all take your seats," the master of ceremonies announced from the podium. Jim and I made our way up to the podium to welcome everyone. I could feel my mouth move as the words tumbled out, but I felt as if I were a bystander watching everything happen from an obscure corner.

After we sat back down, my mother leaned over toward me.

"They're going to show a video of Hunter. Are you sure you're ready for this?" my mother tenderly whispered to me.

"I'm fine," I assured her weakly; my voice muffled, buried beneath a fierce landslide of grief-laden memories. I longed to leave but knew I had to stay—if not for anyone else but the girls. I didn't want them to think something was wrong—

even though everything was. Hunter had not been gone that long, and though I was doing the best I could to stay afloat, I was taking on water and sinking fast. I fell into a silent daze as I sat crumpled in my chair. Suddenly, I knew I had to escape—I wasn't going to make it through the event. "I need to leave. I need to leave right now, Mom. Will you stay with the girls?" I wanted out of there so badly, and ran as fast as I could back to our hotel room.

Bursting into the bedroom, I grabbed my luggage from the corner of the room where I had tucked it and whipped it open. Clothes flew everywhere as I tore the place apart searching for my toiletry bag. Upon finding the culprit, I rummaged through it until I found relief; the sleeping pills and anti-anxiety pills that had become my temporary lifeline. Quickly tearing open both containers, I poured as many as I could hold in the palm of my hand. Pills fell and scattered across the floor as I reached for the bottled water sitting on the nightstand.

I slammed myself into the bed and buried my face into the coverlet screaming, "God, what do you want from me?" as loud as I could. My throat burned and my head throbbed as I continued to sob convulsively, screaming at the top of my lungs. Roots of despair snaked their way deep into my tortured soul, causing me to summon every ounce of strength I had to put the pills back where they belonged.

An abrupt knock on the door broke the spell and snapped me out of my trance, leading me to swiftly dump the pills back into the toiletry bag. Peering through the peephole in the door, I breathed an embarrassed sigh of relief upon seeing my mother's concerned eyes searching for me. She's come to my rescue yet again.

This moment hangs the darkness out there so explicitly that I wasn't sure if I should even share it with you. It chronicles my complete collapse beneath the weight of a grief far too intense to bear, though thankfully my actual implosion was behind closed doors. The destructive nature of what I almost did that night, trapped in the jaws of despair, screams evil.

It was close to nine months after Hunter went to heaven. I had fallen into a deep, ugly abyss about a month before this hotel room meltdown, though I managed to keep most of what I was going through undercover for the sake of the girls. I didn't want them to worry or feel like they were losing their mother when the pain of losing their brother was still so fresh.

While most of what I had experienced was part of the normal grief process, this moment was the closest I came to actually giving up the fight and acting on my feelings. That night in the hotel room, when choking darkness billowed over my soul, I had absolutely no control over the lies and fear stalking my mind, body, and spirit. Honestly, I felt as if my only hope lay in death.

Unfortunately, my desolation didn't end after my mother rescued me. Like a hurricane, it continued to strengthen, the fury of its doubt hammering my faith relentlessly, eroding it like a storm surge wears away the beauty of the coastline. The temptation to reject the Word of God and buy in to the lie that God had abandoned me was overwhelming. So much so that I actually began to believe that I was no longer His. It scared me to death. Literally.

At the time, my grief was so crippling that it undermined my ability to reason and believe. Somehow I began to swallow the lie that death was a legitimate course of action, a game changer, an escape. Certainly part of what I was experiencing was the deep anguish of soul over the loss of my precious son, but there was more going on. Would this longing for death actually help me die more to myself, bringing about less of me and more of Christ? Or was this just another way to overspiritualize my desperation so I might come out smelling like a spiritual rose?

What I didn't realize at the time was that my spiritual pride had me thinking that a good/strong Christian should never be depressed— even if her son died. While I had recently started my antidepressant and anti-anxiety meds, I did so reluctantly, under protest, because I was concerned about the opinions of others. Needless to say, at the time of the hotel room moment, they had not kicked in, and any therapeutic virtue was obviously yet to be realized. I had been strong in my faith and keenly aware that people were watching, acknowledging my strength in the Lord. Consequently, when this episode unfolded and I found myself lost in the Valley of the Shadow, I became more concerned about people seeing me so frail and weak than following God humbly through it. I fought what God was providing through medical help in the most spiritual terms in which I could frame my stubborn heart. Eventually, I had to get real and die to my pride and spiritual posturing, despite how ugly "real" appeared. The net effect was that I came out of the experience with a greater boldness to share the gospel because I realized its power in a deeper way. You see, in all of this I learned that it's not about trusting the level of faith we have in the Lord in the moment—it's simply about His faithfulness. It's not about faith in faith, but faith in His faithfulness that leads to full surrender. As much as the enemy sought to tempt me, God made a promise— He's faithful even when I'm not. My faith in Christ wasn't going to be the rescue; *Jesus was and is the rescue.*

We wonder, "Is God going to take care of me? Does He see what I'm going through? If He loves me, doesn't He want better for me?" Bottom line, we doubt God and His perfect love for us. It's almost like we're fighting *against* who He is, the promises He has made, and the truth He has revealed about Himself through His Word.

And though the battle rages hot and fierce, our hope in temptation is this: a way out. Through gracious provision, God in His immeasurable mercy made a way out for us through Jesus. Our life circumstances may be beyond our ability to endure, but they're no match for God. *He* is our hope. Every time. Not sometimes. Not when we feel strong enough. Not when we're at the top of our game.

Every.

Single.

Time.

As sure as the night falls, overwhelming the light of day, we *will* be tempted—it's a given. Tempted to trust in, hope in, and flat-out invest our heart and soul in everyone and everything *except* God. When, like Peter, we don't want to die to something or lose something, we cry out, "Lord, may this cross be far from You" but really mean, "Lord, may this cross be far from *me*." We can count on this temptation. But we can also count on God's love that beckons us to new life built on promises He doesn't just make—but keeps!

It's a certainty that the enemy of our soul wants to ruin our lives and will tempt us at every twist, turn, and fork in the road. However, as sure as the waves of circumstance will try to pull us under and sweep us out to seas of despair, God promises to break their undertow and lead us to shores of peace in His steadfast love and lasting faithfulness. My own journey to the brink of despair at the hands of my weakness and anguish turned out to result not only in my deliverance, but a depth of faith in the love of God I could not have known any other way.

God knows our human frailties, and because He knows, we can trust Him with every circumstance we face. In Christ, the crisis and temptation to doubt actually work for us instead of against us. When Christ is our all-consuming satisfaction, He helps us to die to that which is not of Him—to the very things that nailed Him to the cross in the first place. The penalty and burden of the corruption and sin that so easily entangles us was satisfied on the cross through His death. The fear and dread of death was taken care of once for all. Jesus died and rose again so we can die too—even to death, because perfect love casts out all fear, including our fear of death.

I think John Piper summarized best what I'm trying to say here:

> The life of a Christian includes many deaths. Paul said, "I die every day!" (1 Corinthians 15:31). Jesus said, "If anyone would come after me, let him deny himself and take up his cross daily and follow me" (Luke 9:23). Daily Christian living is daily Christian dying. The dying I have in mind is the dying of comfort and security and reputation and health and family and friends and wealth and homeland. These may be taken from us at any time in the path of Christ-exalting obedience. To die daily the way Paul did, and to take up our cross daily the way Jesus commanded is to embrace the life of loss for Christ's sake and count it gain.
>
> In other words, the way we honor Christ in death is to treasure Jesus above the gift of life, and the way we honor Christ in life is to treasure Jesus above life's gifts.[2]

The fire's dying. It needs another log or two. But maybe not... You know, there's nothing like a roaring fire dancing about the hearth, but the beauty of the embers as the flames wither remains unrivaled to me. Like autumn's blazing colors that burst and pass as they herald the beauty in death, these poetic embers warm my heart in a way its frolicking flames never could.

I think if fire could speak, or maybe if we could understand its language, we would discover that it, like so much in nature, embraces the path it must take. The one it was created for. From small, faltering beginnings to raging inferno to embers and finally ashes, it doesn't fight its four seasons but is happily spent in its destiny.

How about you? Do you fight tomorrow, the unknown, the future? Are you ready and willing to pass from time into eternity? Do you understand that if you know Christ when you close your eyes here, you will open them in paradise, to the waiting, loving arms of Jesus? Have you received forgiveness and spiritual wholeness that can only be found through a Savior? Have you fully surrendered your life to His Lordship and received His Spirit in your heart? Have you been born again from above? You can if you're willing to turn from all that separates you from His love, mercy, and grace. Wouldn't you rather embrace the life you were created and destined for? Remember this, any way you cut it, if you try to save your life, you will lose it (see Matt. 16:25). Whoever dies with the most toys...

...is still dead.

Ultimately, until we discover someone or something worth dying for, we can never really live. The conviction created through knowing what you would die for makes you more alive. You've got a reason to risk everything—something more valuable, greater than you and your life...a message greater than the messenger! It births a willingness and passion to venture out of your comfort zone, stand on the edge of the cliff— do things that fear has kept you from. Things like preaching the gospel in a foreign land where they'll kill you if they catch you. Be a voice for those who don't have one. Live without luxury to bring the good news to those who have no hope. Live unchained so you can bring the truth to those in bondage. Surrender your rights and all claims to this life for the sake of His righteousness.

And so I have to ask, if you're a believer, are you denying yourself, taking up *your* cross, dying daily to your desires and dreams, to the things of this world—that you might walk in His greater dream and desire for you right now and His perfect promises for all eternity? Remember, if so, then rest assured that when that day comes and you pass from this world to the next, it's just a step from time into the timeless. From the darkness of this decadent, fallen, fading race to the light of His eternal love and amazing grace. I can hardly wait. And every time the sun goes down, it's one step closer to that day.

Being ever mindful of this, I thank Him for this day, this moment, and the promise of the joy that's set before us. It all speaks life and inspires us to press on with passion as the great cloud of witnesses (that includes my son) cheers us on from heaven.

What to Remember and Never Forget...

- We have a choice: will we die right along with the world and its passing pleasures, or will we die to it and live for Him where the greater treasure is because He is our great reward?
- In facing death we often reflect upon life, so the idea that "you don't know what you've got until it's gone" becomes deeply impacting as we get up close and personal with death.
- The fear and dread of death was taken care of once for all. Jesus died and rose again so that we can die too—even to death, because perfect love casts out all fear, including our fear of death.
- Any way you cut it, if you try to save your life, you will lose it (see Matt. 16:25)—whoever dies clinging to the most toys is still dead.

Prayer...

My God, the instinct for self-preservation might as well have put the hammer and nails that killed You in my hands. I long to die to this life and live unto You in Your resurrection life—help me embrace the grace to do just that. Help me live eternally through time, and die to the toys, promises, and lies that this world so easily sells me that I might glorify You and walk in eternal life to-

day. Help me to live all in—with passion for the sake of Your Name and all that is Yours. Where there is any trace of fear trying to hold me back from a sold-out life, please conquer it with Your perfect love. In Jesus' matchless name and victory I pray.

    ~Amen!

Truths about Death to Etch Upon Your Heart:

And anyone who does not take his cross and follow me is not worthy of me. Whoever finds his life will lose it, and whoever loses his life for my sake will find it. (Matthew 10:38–39)

And anyone who does not carry his cross and follow me cannot be my disciple. (Luke 14:27)

In the same way, any of you who does not give up everything he has cannot be my disciple. (Luke 14:33)

For we know that our old self was crucified with him so that the body of sin might be done away with, that we should no longer be slaves to sin—because anyone who has died had been freed from sin. Now if we died with Christ, we believe that we will also live with him. For we know that since Christ was raised from the dead, he cannot die again; death no longer has mastery over him. The death he died, he died to sin once for all; but the life he lives; he lives to God. (Romans 6:6–10)

Therefore we do not lose heart. Though outwardly we are wasting away, yet inwardly we are being renewed day by day. For our light and momentary troubles are achieving for us an eternal glory that far outweighs them all. So we fix our eyes not on what is seen, but on what is unseen. For what is seen is temporary, but what is unseen is eternal. (2 Corinthians 4:16–18)

I have been crucified with Christ and I no longer live, but Christ lives in me. The life I live in the body, I live by faith in the Son of God, who loved me and gave himself for me. (Galatians 2:20)

Those who belong to Christ Jesus have crucified the sinful nature with its passions and desires. (Galatians 5:24)

For to me, to live is Christ and to die is gain. (Philippians 1:21)

Set your minds on things above, not on earthly things. For you died, and your life is now hidden with Christ in God. (Colossians 3:2–3) *one more thing before you go*

You need to go and find twelve stones. I'm not kidding. Stop reading, go outside and find twelve stones. I'll be waiting right here for you, so go ahead—go. (Can you tell that I'm a firstborn? Yikes. You'll have to forgive me for that—even though birth order is a God thing.) Mine are sitting here on the table to the right of my computer. All piled up in a shot glass (yes, we used to use shot glasses for lesser purposes), they will forever be a visual reminder of this journey for me. I have to laugh because it's snowing here, so as you might imagine, gathering these stones was no easy task. But that's good and I'll tell you why in a minute.

Did you get your twelve stones? I hope so, because I want you to remember what I'm about to share with you, and it's important for you to have a visual reminder of this next story. It's been a hard blessing pouring out the moments I've shared with you in the midst of these pages. If words could convey the depth of what this has been like, I would use them. But words fall short, and I suppose they should. So in closing I'd like to leave you with a few stories that are not my own—yet they are. Although I didn't experience these moments, they are just as much a part of my story as they are yours.

After wandering in the desert wilderness because of sin and disobedience, God's people were finally prepared and ready to enter the land He had promised them. Handpicked by God, Joshua would lead His people, Israel, into the long-awaited and eagerly anticipated land of milk and honey. The promise given decades before to Abraham and his descendants and passed down to Moses (and to you and me—but we'll get to that in a minute) would finally come to fruition. It was the moment they'd all been waiting and praying for.

The story begins in the book of Joshua.

> After the death of Moses the servant of the LORD, the LORD said to Joshua son of Nun, Moses' aide: "Moses my servant is dead. Now then, you and all these people, get ready to cross the Jordan River into the land I am about to give to them—the Israelites. I will give you every place where you set your foot, as I promised Moses.... No one will be able to stand up against you all the days of your life. As I was with Moses, so I will be with you; I will never leave you nor forsake you.
>
> "Be strong and courageous, because you will lead these people to inherit the land I swore to their forefathers to give them. Be strong and very courageous. Be careful to obey all the law my servant Moses gave you; do not turn from it to the right or to the left, that you may be successful wherever you go. Do not let this Book of the Law depart from your mouth; meditate on it day and night,

so that you may be careful to do everything written in it. Then you will be prosperous and successful. Have I not commanded you? Be strong and courageous, for the LORD your God will be with you wherever you go."

So Joshua ordered the officers of the people: "Go through the camp and tell the people, 'Get your supplies ready. Three days from now you will cross the Jordan here to go in and take possession of the land the LORD your God is giving you for your own.'" (Joshua 1:1–3, 5–11)

For three days God readied them for the crossing, for the miracle and the remembering. And then it happened.

Joshua said to the Israelites, "Come here and listen to the words of the LORD your God. This is how you will know that the living God is among you and that he will certainly drive out before you the Canaanites, Hittites, Hivites, Perizzites, Girgashites, Amorites and Jebusites. See, the ark of the covenant of the Lord of all the earth will go into the Jordan ahead of you. Now then, choose twelve men from the tribes of Israel, one from each tribe. And as soon as the priests who carry the ark of the LORD—the Lord of all the earth—set foot in the Jordan, its waters flowing downstream will be cut off and stand in a heap."

So when the people broke camp to cross the Jordan, the priests carrying the ark of the covenant went ahead of them. Now the Jordan is at flood stage all during harvest. Yet as soon as the priests who carried the ark reached the Jordan and their feet touched the water's edge, the water from upstream stopped flowing. It piled up in a heap a great distance away, at a town called Adam in the vicinity of Zarethan, while the water flowing down to the Sea of the Arabah (the Salt Sea) was completely cut off. So the people crossed over opposite Jericho. The priests who carried the ark of the covenant of the LORD stood firm on dry ground in the middle of the Jordan, while all Israel passed by until the whole nation had completed the crossing on dry ground. (Joshua 3:9–17)

I need to interrupt this incredible story for a minute. I've read this story a number of times, but God has moved my heart to see and share an incredible picture of His grace that I had never seen before. The people in the town called Adam in the vicinity of Zarethan—people not part of His chosen tribe of Jacob, Israel, but Gentiles, not descendants of Abraham—these people got to witness the miracle too. Can you even imagine? Let's try. You're walking to the well to get some water to cook dinner. It's an ordinary day. The sun beats warm upon your face. It's been a typical back-breaking day and you're already exhausted, really not looking forward to cooking for the family. And then it happens. You hear a thunderous noise growing louder and louder and look up to see a towering wall of water rushing down the river and pooling like a foaming, fluid mountain. A majestic prism, it blocks the sky, causing sunlight to break into a vibrant rainbow that reaches across the landscape with its magnificent colors. You're terrified. The water cistern shatters into a thousand pieces as you drop it and run to fetch your children. It's a miracle.

I'll try not to get too carried away, and as you know there's no seminary degree hanging on my wall but I can't help but see us (you and me) in the town of Adam (interesting name, don't you think?). We are the Gentiles watching this miracle unfold through God's boundless grace—we've been grafted in, set apart, chosen. Not because of anything we've done, but because of Him. Just like the people in the town of Adam.

They never deserved the miracle; they weren't God's chosen people, but they witnessed the miracle, and I imagine it was a moment they remembered and never forgot.

Thank you for sidetracking with me, now let's get back to the story. Miraculously, the Israelites cross the Jordan on dry ground and now God pulls Joshua aside for another message for His people. But I think this one is for you and for me too, so let's listen up.

> When the whole nation had finished crossing the Jordan, the LORD said to Joshua, "Choose twelve men from among the people, one from each tribe, and tell them to take up twelve stones from the middle of the Jordan from right where the priests stood and to carry them over with you and put them down at the place where you stay tonight."
>
> So Joshua called together the twelve men he had appointed from the Israelites, one from each tribe, and said to them, "Go over before the ark of the LORD your God into the middle of the Jordan. Each of you is to take up a stone on his shoulder, according to the number of the tribes of the Israelites, to serve as a sign among you. In the future, when your children ask you, 'What do these stones mean?' tell them that the flow of the Jordan was cut off before the ark of the covenant of the LORD. When it crossed the Jordan, the waters of the Jordan were cut off. These stones are to be a memorial to the people of Israel forever."
>
> So the Israelites did as Joshua commanded them. They took twelve stones from the middle of the Jordan, according to the number of the tribes of the Israelites, as the LORD had told Joshua; and they carried them over with them to their camp, where they put them down. Joshua

set up the twelve stones that had been in the middle of the Jordan at the spot where the priests who carried the ark of the covenant had stood. And they are there to this day. (Joshua 4:1–9)

God wants us to remember and never forget...

What will your twelve stones represent? In the future when your children see your twelve stones and ask you, "What do these stones mean?" what will you tell them? What do they mean?

The God of Abraham, Moses, and Joshua is the same God yesterday, today, and forever. Just as He was with Joshua, He is with you. Right now. In the midst of the moments—that's what the twelve stones represent for me. Moments. Moments that I love to remember and moments I wish I could forget. Moments covered in shame, guilt, and sin. Moments drenched in tears of sorrow, anguish, and grief. Unforgettable moments, too good to be true—bursting with joy and alive with meaning. And all of the other God-moments in between.

I remember the moments because they've become part of His message.

Twelve stones that represent the deep scars and sweet satisfaction of a life of moments lived for the Savior. A Savior whose scars are a visual reminder for us—a reminder of the great cost of redemption and His willingness to pay the ultimate price. Each stone and scar beautiful. Carved out and plucked up from hardened ground for a purpose and plan immeasurably greater than I could ever ask or imagine. A reminder of what made this woman desperate for Jesus. And hopefully a life that reflects Him more and more with each passing moment.

What will you allow Jesus to do in your heart and life right now in this moment etched in time for all eternity? Are you getting ready to walk through the Jordan on dry ground to head into the promised land God has prepared for you? Are you hoping, praying, and believing? Do you hear the love in these encouraging words from your Heavenly Father, "Be strong and courageous. Do not be terrified; do not be discouraged, for the LORD your God will be with you wherever you go"?

Are you ready to pick up the stones from the moments of your life thus far? Are you ready to lay them down as a memorial of what the Lord has done in your life, in the midst of the moments you remember—so you'll never forget?

I have my shot glass of stones but I also have my journals, "trust Jesus" notes from Erin, photographs, cards, and letters all to remind me, because I will forget what God has done and so will you. How do I know this? Well, all you have to do is read some history; open your Bible. Here's just a taste of what I'm referring to. This story is found in the Old Testament book of Psalms:

> They forgot what he had done, the wonders he had shown them. He did miracles in the sight of their fathers in the land of Egypt, in the region of Zoan. He divided the sea and led them through; he made the water stand firm like a wall. He guided them with the cloud by day and with the light from the fire all night. He split the rocks in the desert and gave them water as abundant as the seas; he brought streams out of a rocky crag and made waters flow down like rivers. But they continued to sin against him, rebelling in the desert against the Most High. They willfully put God to the test by demanding the food they craved. They spoke against God, saying, "Can God spread a table in the desert? When he struck the rock, water gushed out, and streams flowed abundantly. But can he also give us food? Can he supply meat for his people?" (Psalm 78:11–20)

This all happened after God parted the Red Sea. *He. Parted. The. Red. Sea.* Right in front of them. They walked through the sea on dry ground, walls of water towering on each side of them. Are you kidding me? How could they forget what the Lord did for them? And then He sent them manna from heaven and water from a rock. What? Food from heaven. Water from a rock. Seriously, I don't know about you but I can't imagine getting over eating a feast delivered from the hand of God. Certainly, it had to be better than McDonald's.

How could they forget what He did?

How can we?

The forgetfulness of God's people is etched all through the pages of Scripture. But let's not be so quick to throw them under the bus, because the truth is, we're just like them. We forget. We forget what God has done in our lives. We forget the moments where He so clearly displayed His love and faithfulness. We move on and start complaining about everything that's wrong while forgetting about everything He has done. We get caught up in our many plans and forget that His purpose will always prevail. We plead and pray and He answers in the most incredible way, but then the cares of this world distract us again and we forget to thank Him for coming to the rescue. We forget!

But He never does.

God never forgets His people.

He's always and forever faithful. Though we forget, He will never forget us.

Again let me ask, what will your twelve stones represent? When your friends and family see them gathering dust on your desk, on your dresser, or even in your car and ask what you're doing with a little pile of stones, your answer is, "These stones mean..."

What? What do these stones mean? What is it that God has done, that He wants you to personally remember and never forget? To memorialize? What is the Jordan River in your life that God has parted against all odds to usher you into your promised land at this time, in this place? And how will these stones serve to inspire you today for something done yesterday? What's this living connection that awakens the present through the past? Yes, we need to remember how far we have come, the depths from which God has rescued us, but God's not interested in becoming a memory. He wants full on in the right now—this moment! He carried you this far, into this moment, this "right now." Every circumstance, trial, tear, and triumph have been part of the "working all things together for good" plan of God. Will you allow these lifeless stones to be an echo of these words, brimming with life, "Be strong and courageous. Do not be terrified; do not be discouraged, for the LORD your God will be with you wherever you go."

Let me ask you one last time, what will your twelve stones represent?

afterword

*M*aybe not today, and probably not tomorrow either, but…someday! Someday you'll be thankful for the very moments that made you hurt the most! Most of the moments that I've shared with you hurt a lot. Actually, that's not quite true—they didn't just hurt, they devastated me to the core! But now I can look back at each and every moment I spent in the fires of adversity through the eyes of redemption and grace…

And I thank God.

I thank Him for shattering the picture of the perfect family—because perfection is a facade apart from the Perfect One. I thank Him for allowing me to seek after *love* in all the wrong places and faces—because in finding what love is not, I have found Love Himself. I thank Him for

allowing me to squander myself in trying to be who I thought I was supposed to be—because in knowing Him and all that He is, I'm free to be
all that He created me to be. I thank Him for letting me taste and see
the treasures of this world—because now I know that He alone is my
greatest treasure and reward. I thank Him for allowing my one and only
son, Hunter, to suffer (as painful as that was)—because through his *suffering* I have found the Savior, God's One and Only Son, whose suffering
changed everything.

I thank Him for the mess that *was* my life because it has become part
of His message of life.

It all matters. Every experience . . .

Every tear.

Every joy.

Every mountain.

Every valley.

Every bright spot.

Every shadow.

Every.

Moment.

Matters.

Why? Because He was there. In the midst of it all, God was there
orchestrating every single detail of your story and mine, weaving every
moment into the more beautiful tapestry—the greater story. The story
that started before time was established, when God already had a plan
for you and me in mind. He's the Beginning and the End, the architect
of every moment and every destiny.

These words may seem trite or even unrealistic in the face of extreme
misfortune and severe hardship. It's easy for me to say—I don't know
what you're going through, what you've endured, or what losses you may
have suffered. What I do know from experience, however, is that God is
faithful to His own love. That He never afflicts willingly, yet will make
the tough, tough calls if it's ultimately for His glory and our highest

good. And He feels every hurt we feel, suffers each and every disappointment, heartbreak, agony, and grief that we do—we do not suffer alone.
He weeps with us, yet who dries *His* tears?

And from the ashes of our crushed hopes He crowns us with
beauty, from the depths of our mourning He lifts our hearts in joy,
and in the stark chill of our despair He wraps us warmly in praise.
No, I have not felt the sting of the deaths you have died, the fires of
adversity that left your dreams smoldering in their wake, or the desolation of soul you've curled up with…but neither have you felt mine.
What matters most is the fact that He knows and cares deeply—
enough to not only do something about our heartbreak, but actually
use it to heal us!

It may not be today, and it may not be tomorrow—but someday
you'll be thankful for the very moments that made you hurt the most.
For it's your sorrow that will lead you to His love, and your suffering
that will bring you to His grace. Were it not for them, you'd continue to
wander blindly through your wasteland of self-sufficiency and pretense,
thinking you were flying while all the time…

You were falling.

And you know that what they say is true, it's not the fall…

It's the landing that kills you.

Wouldn't you rather soar on the wings of His redemption and
restoration?

Wouldn't you rather fall into the arms of the One who knows and
loves you always and forever—no matter what?

So here we are at the end of our time together. The fire has dwindled
to smoldering ashes in the hearth, but my heart is on fire, ablaze with
gratitude, anticipation, and excitement.

Because I'm ready.

Ready for the next moment.

The one that God has already prepared in advance for me to walk
into.

Each moment flowing into the next, emptying into the depths of a vast lasting legacy, reflecting the radiance of His love etched upon my heart. A perfect picture of the Father's heart, the way it really is—and the way I long for it to be.

Are you with me?

gratitude

*I thank my God every time I remember you.
In all my prayers for all of you, I always pray
with joy because of your partnership in the
gospel from the first day until now.*

Philippians 1:3–5

Writing a book humbles you, especially a book like this. But even more humbling is the beauty of God bringing together people for a purpose far beyond anything we could imagine or dream. That's what this journey has been like—a coming together of the chosen to comfort others with the extravagant comfort we've all received through Christ.

My heart overflows with a gratitude that words can never contain or explain. But words are all that I can give on this page, so please receive them and know that what I wish to say, words would never be able to convey. Who am I that God would surround me with such incredibly gifted, God-honoring people? I thank Him for the privilege of working with individuals that first and foremost know and love Him—but that also seek to make *Him* known.

to my mother . . . You listened, wiped tears, prayed, fasted, nudged me, and picked me up when I couldn't get off the floor. In my writing wilderness you were the one crying in the desert with me, encouraging me to press on and into the promised land. I'll never understand why God would bless me with such an incredible mother, friend, and mentor. Thank you for always believing, hoping, and loving. Love you MORE!

to my dad...Thank you for being willing and vulnerable to let God use you in this way. I see Jesus in you more and more every day. I love you—always have and always will.

to my girls...Words will never hold my love for you and your brother, Hunter. It will always be MORE, MORE...MORE! Thank you for praying, fasting, and loving me as I poured my heart into this book. This is all for you—so that you'll learn, grow, and always remember and never forget how amazing God really is. He loves you like crazy...and so do I. Erin—you're already a gifted writer and editor. I can't wait to see how God will continue to use your gifts for His glory and kingdom. Cam—you have blessed countless girls through *Hot Chocolate with God*; Jesus is being magnified through you! You go, girl!

to Daddy, JK...Once again, your willingness to be vulnerable and open humbles and blesses me beyond measure. Thank you for praying, for being patient and understanding, for listening to Christian music even when I wasn't in the car, for being who you are—because who you are is such a wondrous gift to me. I love you!

to my faithful "wingman"—Rick Kern...I can't write without you—and that pretty much covers it. You're a maestro with words, creating beautiful music with words, sentences, and paragraphs. And yet, your writing gift is just a bonus. You're a man of strong faith, integrity, and character. A faithful prayer warrior and trusted friend. Thank you for everything. P.S. I still think you need to get emoticons.

to Jana...I love you, my friend! I thank God for allowing our paths to cross at just the right time. He's so good! Your friendship is a gift, and the fact that you love football is a huge bonus! Thank you for believing in the heart and hope of this book. Your patience, persistence, and passion have blessed me. Tell Kenzie the Kelly girls are coming for a visit.

to Robert Wolgemuth and your gifted team...To think that our Chichi Bella was the first to know...You're special, hand-picked by God for such a time as this to brave the literary world on behalf of Team Kelly—thank you! I can't imagine traveling this road without you!

to *Patti*...You're always there for me. Thank you for carving out the time to read, edit, laugh, and cry with me. You're incredibly gifted in so many ways. I can't wait to see what God will do with all He has given you. Love you!

to *my sister-in-law Kim*...I love you! Thank you for praying and always encouraging me. I thank God for blessing my brother and our family with you.

to *Pastor Deone Drake*...Because of your passion for Jesus and His Word, I long to know Him more. I thank God for your example and sold-out witness for the sake of Christ. Thank you for taking the time to read this work.

to *my faithful friends/prayer warriors (JK Fellowship, Katherine, Sassy, and the Giggly Glory Girls, Katie Almy, Matt and Kelsey Gold, Pat and Rita Curtin, Coach Sam and Marcus, Mooch and Shellie, Nancy, Joanne, Jessica, Karen K., LaDonna, Mary McGuire, Connie, Cassie, Kendra Moore, Shelly Wilson, Lisa Whittle, the Hunter's Hope staff, Facebook and Twitter friends...and the rest of my dear friends)*...Your willingness to bend the knee for me during this writing journey means more than words can convey. I pray that God would pour forth a blessing upon each of your lives, one that is abundant, outrageous, and beyond anything you could ever ask or imagine. Thank you for holding me up!

to *Kristin and Rob*...I thank God for you—your willingness and bravery to share your amazing story is courageous and admirable. I trust that lives will continue to be changed as you both step out in faith and share what God has done.

Lastly...*to Jesus*...Before a word is on my tongue you know it completely, so I'll let my words be few—YOU are everything! I pray my tears are a sweet offering. For King and Kingdom! Come, Lord Jesus!

appendix a

hunter's hope foundation

Hunter's Hope Foundation was created to confront the critical need for information, awareness, and research in response to the threat of Krabbe disease and related leukodystrophies. In addition, we strive to undergird and inspire Krabbe families as they adjust to the extreme demands of living with a terminal illness.

Our Mission

1. To broaden public awareness of Krabbe disease and other leukodystrophies, thus increasing the odds of early detection and treatment.
2. To mount an aggressive public relations campaign throughout political, corporate, and private sectors in hopes of alerting key community leaders to the potential of newborn screening as a weapon in the fight against Krabbe disease.
3. To fund research efforts that will identify and develop new treatments, therapies, and ultimately a cure for Krabbe disease and related leukodystrophies.

4. To establish an alliance of hope that will reach out to those directly and indirectly affected by leukodystrophies, while addressing their urgent need for medical, financial, informational, and emotional support.

Among the primary goals of founders Jim and Jill Kelly is a hands-on appreciation for all children, along with a thankful heart toward God for these precious gifts of life. These bedrock ideals are vigilantly expressed throughout all the foundation's programs and activities.

Core Values

To remain true to and passionate about our bedrock principles.

To be sure our family-oriented, wholesome public image is simply a clear reflection of who we are privately.

To always value individual contributions and never take another's sacrifice for granted, no matter how large or small.

To pursue personal and professional integrity in all matters.

To hold the right of privacy of all individuals in the highest regard.

What Is Universal Newborn Screening?

Universal Newborn Screening is a state-based public health system that is essential for preventing the devastating consequences of a number of medical conditions not clinically recognizable at birth. All babies born in the United States receive newborn screening, yet not all babies are screened for the same diseases. Because the newborn screening requirements differ from state to state and are not universal, children are not being checked for many rare diseases.

Thousands and thousands of babies are born every day in the United States. Most babies appear healthy at birth, full of life and possibility. Yet they could be hiding a rare or potentially devastating disease. By screening every baby at birth, we can prevent serious mental or physical disabilities, even death. Also, by making the requirement universal in every state, we can ensure that no child will have to suffer unnecessarily.

To learn more about Hunter's Hope, Krabbe disease, or Universal Newborn Screening, visit our website, www.huntershope.org.

appendix b

16 things i think jesus would want you to know on your 16th birthday, erin marie kelly

1. *You are loved:* Unconditionally, fully, more than you know, always…no matter what. Nothing can separate you from His love. Nothing!

    > For I am convinced that neither death nor life, neither angels or demons, neither the present nor the future, nor any powers, neither height nor depth, nor anything else in all creation, will be able to separate us from the love of God that is in Christ Jesus our Lord. (Romans 8:37–39)

2. *Because you are loved, Jesus wants to be your first love:* No other love will satisfy your heart—so seek to love Him more every day.

    > Love the LORD your God with all your heart and with all your soul and with all your strength. (Deuteronomy 6:5)

3. *Every time you look in the mirror, remember...you were created for a purpose:* Jesus has a plan and purpose for your life that is unique to you. No one can be you. Therefore, no one can fulfill the purpose for which God has created you.

> And we know that in all things God works for the good of those who love Him, who have been called according to his purpose. (Romans 8:28)

> Many are the plans in a man's heart, but it is the LORD'S purpose that prevails. (Proverbs 19:21)

4. *He is sovereign:* Jesus has orchestrated all the details of your life. Though you may not understand His ways, He is perfect and His good plans for you will prevail. He already knows what your future holds, so don't worry about it...just follow Him and He will lead you right into all that He has for you.

> For you have been my hope, Sovereign LORD, my confidence since my youth. From birth I have relied on you; you brought me forth from my mother's womb. I will ever praise You. (Psalm 71:5–6)

5. *You are never alone:* He is always with you—always.

> The LORD himself goes before you and will be with you; he will never leave you nor forsake you. Do not be afraid; do not be discouraged. (Deuteronomy 31:8)

6. *You are limited but He is limitless:* You can do all things through Christ who strengthens you.

He is the image of the invisible God, the firstborn over all creation. For by him all things were created; things in heaven and on earth, visible and invisible, whether thrones or powers or rulers or authorities; all things were created by him and for him. He is before all things, and in him all things hold together. (Colossians 1:15–17)

7. *You are beautiful*: With a heart for Jesus, your outer beauty radiates even more. When you look in the mirror, remember that God sees beautiful…He made you exactly how He wanted you to be.

> The LORD does not look at the things man looks at. Man looks at the outward appearance, but the LORD looks at the heart. (1 Samuel 16:7)

8. *Put your expectations in Jesus alone*: People will let you down, but He won't. When you put your hope and faith in Jesus, you can expect Him to fulfill His plan—and you will not be disappointed.

> And hope does not disappoint us, because God has poured out his love into our hearts by the Holy Spirit, whom he has given us. (Romans 5:5)

9. *You are forgiven*: For all you have done—past, present, future—you are forgiven. You don't have to try to be good enough…or earn your way to God. Jesus loves you and He has already forgiven you for all that separated you from Him. So don't carry around unforgiveness…forgive everyone, every time, just as Jesus has forgiven you.

> In him we have redemption through his blood, the forgiveness of sins, in accordance with the riches of

God's grace that he lavished on us with all wisdom
and understanding. (Ephesians 1:7–8)

Bear with each other and forgive whatever grievances
you may have against one another. Forgive as the
Lord forgave you. (Colossians 3:13)

10. *Cry, laugh, scream…run to Him with everything*: If you're sad, tell Him.
If you're confused, frustrated, and angry, run into the arms of Jesus.
If you're thankful or joyful, share it with Him. Jesus loves spending
time with you.

Search me, O God, and know my heart; test me and
know my anxious thoughts. See if there is any offensive way in me, and lead me in the way everlasting.
(Psalm 139:23–24)

11. *Walk by faith—not by sight*: Things will happen in your life that you
will not understand. Jesus wants you to trust that His plan is good
even when it appears otherwise. He is trustworthy and faithful.

Therefore we do not lose heart. Though outwardly we
are wasting away, yet inwardly we are being renewed
day by day. For our light and momentary troubles are
achieving for us an eternal glory that far outweighs
them all. So we fix our eyes not on what is seen, but on
what is unseen. For what is seen is temporary, but what
is unseen is eternal. (2 Corinthians 4:16–18)

12. *Drink a lot of water*: Yes, the good water you have come to love, but
even more so the Living Water, Jesus—the Word. There are treasures in the Bible waiting to be discovered—dive in and drink deep.

"If anyone is thirsty, let him come to me and drink.
Whoever believes in me, as the Scripture has said,
streams of living water will flow from within him."
(John 7:37–38)

13. *Every day is one day closer to seeing Him face to face.*

    Teach us to number our days aright, that we may
    gain a heart of wisdom. (Psalm 90:12)

14. *God has already picked a husband for you*: So you don't have to worry or
    think about it at all (but do pray, of course). Remember, when a girl
    is hidden in Christ—the boy must seek Him in order to find her.

    Do not be anxious about anything, but in everything,
    by prayer and petition, with thanksgiving, present
    your requests to God. And the peace of God, which
    transcends all understanding, will guard your hearts
    and your minds in Christ Jesus. (Philippians 4:6–7)

15. *You are not allowed to text and drive*: Do not follow the driving example
    your parents have been for you. You should not put mascara on
    while driving like your mother does. And you should not listen to
    classic rock music while driving like your father does. (LOL)

    Do not conform any longer to the pattern of this world,
    but be transformed by the renewing of your mind. Then
    you will be able to test and approve what God's will is—
    His good, pleasing and perfect will. (Romans 12:2)

16. *LOVE Jesus—and love life*: You have one life to live for Him...enjoy
    this moment...enjoy being 16 fantastic years old. Enjoy each and

every breath. Live with passion. Find someone (Jesus) worth dying for and live for Him.

> In his hand is the life of every creature and the breath of all mankind. (Job 12:10)

notes

Chapter One: Love

1. Jerry Bridges, *Trusting God* (Colorado Springs: NavPress, 2008), 146.
2. A. W. Tozer, *The Knowledge of the Holy* (New York: HarperCollins, 1961), 98.

Chapter Four: Suffering

1. J. I. Packer, *Knowing God* (Downers Grove, IL: InterVarsity Press, 1973), 97.

Chapter Six: Prayer

Epigraph: Dietrich Bonhoeffer, *The Cost of Discipleship* (New York: Touchstone, 1995), 165.
1. Mark Batterson, *The Circle Maker* (Grand Rapids, MI: Zondervan, 2011), 165.
2. Ibid., 165.
3. Ibid.
4. Ibid., 172.
5. Ibid., 179.
6. Ibid.

7. Oswald Chambers, *If You Will Ask: Reflections on the Power of Prayer* (Grand Rapids, MI: Discovery House Publishers, 1994).

Chapter Eight: Death

Epigraph: John Piper, *Don't Waste Your Life* (Wheaton, IL: Crossway Books, 2003), 63.
1. Centers for Disease Control and Prevention, "Life Expectancy," http://www.cdc.gov/nchs/fastats/lifexpec.htm.
2. Piper, *Don't Waste Your Life*, 71.